Journey Into Dreamtime

MUNYA ANDREWS

First published by Ultimate World Publishing 2019
Copyright © 2019 Munya Andrews

ISBN
Print: 978-1-925884-05-0
Ebook: 978-1-925884-06-7

Cover design: Ultimate World Publishing
Front cover: Munya Andrews. The Wunan, 2010
Back cover: Photo by Deirdre Jones
Layout and typesetting: Ultimate World Publishing
Editor: Srah Yuen, Beverly Boorer

ULTIMATE WORLD
——— PUBLISHING ———

Ultimate World Publishing
Diamond Creek, Victoria
Australia 3089
www.writeabook.com.au

Testimonials

This book is easy to read, introducing philosophies and models for life that will open doors to deeper learning, about ourselves and the possibility of a respectful future for all humanity.

The activities presented at the end of each chapter could be used in schools, in learning circles, in healing circles, as tools in therapeutic processes, taking us into who we are and not what others are making us.

Professor Judy Atkinson
Author, *Trauma Trails, Recreating Song Lines: The Transgenerational Effects of Trauma in Indigenous Australia*

This is an incredible journey into the deeply misunderstood complexity, beauty and genius of Indigenous theosophy, philosophy, ethics and continuing societies. Time and space warp and weave magic over generations of coming into being as human. Along the way, they mark the depth of intelligence so beautifully displayed by Munya Andrews.

The wisdom in the book is offered to all. My challenge to you Reader is to go there. Be changed forever. Just like other great human beings through time, Munya's writing shines a light into the darkness. This is a book for our time. It is long overdue.

John Ley
Actor

A clearly articulated, user-friendly and practical book that will hold pride of place in anyone's home. Andrews explains the sometimes-difficult concept of 'Dreamtime' by first outlining basic concepts. She unpacks and clarifies worldview and creation by using analogies and metaphors to better understand our spirituality. All living symbols are explained – nothing is left to the imagination.

Dr Cindy Solonec
Honorary Research Fellow, University of Western Australia

We are fortunate to be living in Australia with our Aboriginal brothers and sisters who are descendants of one of the oldest continuous cultures on the planet. Yet, how many of us can truly say we know anything about their long and rich culture?

Reading this book was both personally moving for me as well as educational and enlightening. The book offers everyone the opportunity to understand more of the extraordinary wisdom and the practical approach to life of our Indigenous people, and with that understanding, the opportunity to close the gap.

Dr Rosina McAlpine
CEO, *Win Win Parenting*

Dedication

For my people and all beautiful souls to keep the Dreamtime alive.

Table of Contents

Chapter 3

Chapter 4

Chapter 5

Chapter 6

Chapter 7

Chapter 1
What is the Dreamtime?

Rock Painting, Kakadu National Park

Nothing stirs the imagination more than Aboriginal Dreamtime. Everyone wants to know what it is. Its very name is enticing. Wherever I go, people ask, "Munya, what is Dreamtime?" In reply, I recall what an Elder once said, "*Gudia* (white people) ask all the time, what is Dreamtime? This is hard to answer because Dreaming is a *really big thing* for Aboriginal people."

In many ways, asking an Aboriginal person to explain Dreamtime is like asking someone to explain Christianity, Buddhism or Judaism in one hundred words or less. It's no easy task. Like many of the world's religions, it can take a lifetime to learn, but I hope to make that task easier by outlining a few basic concepts.

Dreamtime is an Aboriginal English word used to describe the religion or spirituality of Aboriginal Australians. It is a philosophy, a cosmology, a worldview and a way of life that explains how the world was created and our relationship to each other. While some say it isn't a proper translation of traditional terms like Lalai, Nyitting or Tjurrkupa (pronounced as Djoogaba), I love the term Dreamtime. For me, it conjures up a magical and mysterious world. It aligns perfectly with a common idea in many world religions that God is *unknowable*, beyond words or human understanding. This explains why the Wandjina Beings from the Kimberley are portrayed with no mouths. This is like the Tetragrammaton (the four-letter biblical name YWHW) in Jewish culture, which is a symbol for the God of Israel as his true name is deemed unutterable.

This practice reveals an incredible sense of *awe* and respect for something far greater than ourselves. The Dreamtime approach to describing 'God' or its many gods and goddesses is similar. Sometimes the name is *so* sacred that it is whispered, or else the deity is given a symbol. Names are held in high regard by our people who are aware of the *power* of language. So, Aboriginal people totally understand where Jewish people are coming from using the Tetragrammaton.

Dreamtime 'software'

If Dreamtime doesn't come easily to you, don't worry. You might just be unfamiliar with its software coding. Software? Are we talking computers here? Not exactly.

Joseph Campbell who wrote prolifically on world mythology uses the analogy of computers to better understand how religions work. In *The Power of Mythology*, he says: "Each religion is a kind of software that has its own set of signals and will work. If you begin fooling around with signals that belong to another system of software, they just won't work." [1]

These signals have their own cultural coding or computer programming. So, understanding any religion is all about becoming familiar with its software program, which includes its language and symbols.

This book explores what some of those signals or symbols are to guide you on this journey of understanding. Along the way, we talk about creative ancestors spoken of as Dreaming Beings. These beings are what other people might call gods or goddesses. Although Aboriginal people don't use those terms as such, they are effectively the same. People pray to them, seek their guidance, love and revere them. Some are described as human while others take an animal or plant form. The most significant of all the Creator Beings is the Rainbow Snake. We consider why it is called that and the special role it plays in healing. We explore the connection between animals, humans and plants and what it means to have a certain Dreaming or totem. We look at what Aboriginal 'law' is by contrasting the difference between 'lore' and 'law'. We revisit songlines, sacred sites and what it means to *sing* the land. Finally, we uncover why *all* Aboriginal people are related to each other and the special message this has for humanity. Hopefully by the end, you will have a better understanding of Aboriginal Dreamtime and what it has to offer the world.

Aboriginal Diversity

Aboriginal people in Australia are not a single homogenous group who speak the same language. When people find out just how many tribes or nations there are, most are amazed to discover just how diverse Aboriginal people are. The Indigenous Map of Australia published by AIATSIS (Australian Institute of

Aboriginal and Torres Strait Islander Studies) shows there are up to 250 or so Indigenous nations, each having their own language, their own names and 'country' or tribal lands. When viewing the map for the first time, many people draw comparisons with Europe and say they were unaware of just how many different *countries* or traditional lands they had passed through on their travels throughout Australia.

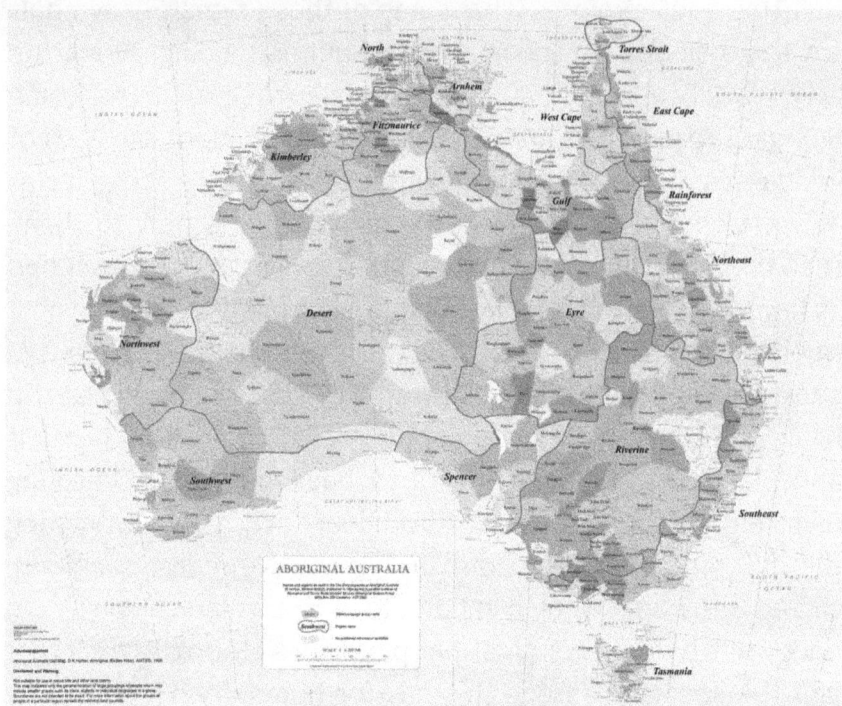

Photo Credit: David R. Horton © 1996

Map of Indigenous Australia

The term 'Aboriginal' is not an Indigenous one. It is a colonial term taken from Latin, which means 'original inhabitant'. Technically speaking, Aboriginal is the adjective whereas Aborigine is the noun. Most Aboriginal people choose to use the adjective rather than the outdated and old fashioned term *Aborigine*. Of course, most prefer their Indigenous names such as Bardi or Bundjalung or pan-Aboriginal names that describe groups identifying with a larger geographical area like Koori for the south-east coast of Australia, Nunga for Aboriginal people living in South Australia or Murri for Indigenous people in Queensland. Pan-Aboriginality asserts a separate national or regional identity not based on traditional ties to land but through association. It came about as a direct result of colonisation where Aboriginal people were forcibly removed from their families and placed on reserves and missions. In the process, many of them lost their language and tribal identity. To assert a distinct Indigenous identity separate from their colonisers, people took on pan-Aboriginal terms like Koori, Nunga and Murri. I use the terms Aboriginal and Indigenous interchangeably along with specific Indigenous names but if in doubt, just follow the adage "When in Rome...." and seek guidance from the local community.

Even though some nations spoke up to five or six surrounding languages, there wasn't a single, mother tongue spoken across Australia. The only languages these nations share today is either English (introduced during Australia's colonial history) or an Aboriginal Kriol known as 'Aboriginal English'. While some individual words are specific to a nation, there are many other common terms that are understood across the country such as 'Dreamtime', 'Dreamings' and 'Songlines'. Although the languages differ completely, they are similar in grammatical construct, pronunciation, sound and syntax. In other words, the arrangement of words and phrases in sentences follows the same structure. Where Dreamtime stories are retold and re-enacted in an Indigenous language, unless fully interpreted, the wisdom contained within remain 'hidden' and localised. Language aside, knowledge is not freely available in Aboriginal culture as it is in western society. There are all sorts of restrictions based on age, clan membership and gender. For example, there are some languages that are only spoken by women and not men, and vice versa. There are also 'inside' and 'outside' languages that pertain to spiritual secrecy, which is discussed in the chapter on Aboriginal Law. But while there is great diversity in the expression of Aboriginal cultures, languages and spirituality, there are some underlying commonalities by way of concepts, principles and themes that we can identify as relating to Dreamtime.

Is ordinary dreaming the same?

People often confuse Dreamtime with ordinary dreaming and sleep time. While dreams *are* a part of the Dreamtime, it is by no means limited to this. Rather, it is an expansive *consciousness* that deals with larger issues such as the meaning of life and everything in between. As Australian anthropologist, Peter Sutton points out, "The use of the English word Dreaming is more a matter of analogy than of translation."[2] Be that as it may, Aboriginal people distinguish between ordinary dreams and those of a more spiritual or Dreamtime nature. For example, the Worora people of the Kimberley refer to ordinary dreaming as *yarri* whereas *buraal* refers to a different kind when one consciously enters another dimension or reality.[3]

Like Aboriginal people, Carl Jung, the father of Jungian psychology, differentiated between these two types, what he called the personal versus the archetypal dream.[4] So too did Joseph Campbell who used the term 'mythic' instead of archetypal.[5] Essentially, they are the same thing. Jung saw these dreams as emerging from our common human experience, what he called the 'collective unconscious'. Buraal or archetypal dreams are sacred because they come from the Dreamtime and are often shared with community members for enlightenment on religious matters whereas yarri dreams are regarded as personal. If you've ever seen the sci-fi movie *Contact* starring Jodie Foster, there is a moment where she loses time when she travels in space and encounters her dead father that she cannot account for. Scientists are quick to dismiss her experience as just a 'dream,' but that scene comes very close to a Dreamtime experience.

Many Aboriginal spiritual epiphanies are shared with other world religions. One example given by Ngarrinyin Elder, David Mowarljarlai involves a Cleverman who encounters a 'book' on his journey to the spiritworld that records all our earthly deeds. "You can't escape your life record," he says.[6] This awareness equates to the *Akashic Records* of Theosophy. There are many other cross-overs between Dreamtime and other religions, which become apparent as you learn more.

What does it mean to have Dreaming?

Another question I'm often asked is: "Munya, what does it mean to have kangaroo, possum or some other Dreaming?" One of the best explanations I've heard is given by Trevor Wie from Darwin who talks about what it means from a practical perspective. Trevor isn't Indigenous but is a fantastic ally to Aboriginal people. He lives and works with our mob in Kakadu and is respected by them. Using a strengths-based approach, he says Dreaming is all about helping people spiritually. It teaches us how to cope with life by identifying the "issues and challenges we need to face" [7]. By learning from our totem, we develop a strong sense of self and well-being so that we can better contribute to society.

Our Dreaming and the stories associated with it help guide us through life. It helps identify those things you need to master to know who you are on life's journey. Through this process of self-discovery, people become aware of their calling or vocation in life. In my Dreamtime teachings, I invite people to discover their personal Dreamings as a source of pride and strength. Once you know what your Dreaming is, "You know who you are and what you are in terms of a symbol," says Wie.[8] This learning may take a lifetime but you're continually refining it throughout your life he says. Ultimately, through their Dreaming, people learn of "the nature of existence which keeps them in a heart-based state." [9]

What is the difference between 'Dreaming' and 'Totem'?

Totem is a Native American term that has been introduced to our language whereas Dreaming comes from Australian Aboriginal culture. However, totem is now used by some Aboriginal people to refer to their Dreaming. Essentially, we're talking about the same principle, the difference being semantic. A *totem* is a spirit being, a sacred object, or symbol that serves as an emblem of a group of people, such as a family, clan, lineage, or tribe. Another Native American term that expresses this idea is 'power animal'. No matter their origin, totems and Dreamings operate in the same way. They provide personal and social identity to an individual or group, they empower people and help us feel more connected to all living and non-living things. Both foster a strong sense of kinship and kindredness that serves to unite us. All cultures understand totems on a heart level, the remnants of which we see in sports teams with their animal mascots such as eagles and bears, or cardinals and coyotes, swans or tigers and so on.

How do you get your Dreaming?

The way in which you get your personal and group Dreaming differs. Your group totem comes from the clan or family you are born into. For example, my Bardi family totem is Nimanburr, which is Flying Fox or Fruit Bat. Another word that our people use for their family or tribe is the Aboriginal English term 'mob', so we refer to ourselves as 'Flying Fox' mob.

Your personal Dreaming, on the other hand, may come about in one or two ways. Either someone knowledgeable (usually an Elder) identifies it for you, or you have an epiphany of your own. You may fly in your dreams, which means you can see the bigger picture in life. Chances are, you have Bird Dreaming of some sort. Or you may be good at working in the background with the finer detail or fly under the radar. In that case, you may have an Insect Dreaming of some kind, such as Ant. If you can't identify specific traits that you relate to, you may notice that you attract a certain animal or bird or object. Can you think of where something has stood out as being odd? Perhaps you've noticed a magpie that regularly visits you or dolphins that always appear when you go swimming in the ocean or crystals you always come across. That would be a good signpost to your Dreaming. Once you have an inkling of what it might be, you might consult an Elder to confirm your feelings or thoughts on the subject. You *can* have more than one or two Dreamings. In my *Dreamtime* workshops, I help people discover what their totems are through meditation and other creative activities. What people experience at these retreats is quite profound and life-changing.

What does my Dreaming teach me?

We also explore the strengths our personal and family Dreamings bring us on our life journey. For example, my Bat totem enables me to see things from a new perspective, especially an upside-down point of view. Whenever I want to look at an issue or problem in a new light, I hang upside down like a bat and can easily see new solutions and possibilities than I am otherwise unable to.

My Nimanburr 'Bat Dreaming'

Bat Dreaming also teaches me about self-care and self-protection in the way that bats envelop themselves in their bat wings. Their heightened sense of sonic hearing teaches me to go beyond the limitations of human hearing, to attune myself to unseen worlds and unsaid words and to listen deeply. I do this through Indigenous practices such as Dadirri (deep listening) that teaches people to do just that using what I call, 'Dreaming Ears'. This is one way in which my family totem or Dreaming helps me cope with life, as Trevor Wie suggests.

My Arlan 'Eagle Dreaming'

My personal Dreaming, on the other hand, is *Arlan* the white chested sea eagle, as opposed to the wedge tail. Eagles fly high in the sky so they can see far and wide. And because they can see the lie of the land, they can see the 'bigger picture'. But when they need to hone in on the finer details, they can do that also. If you have Eagle Dreaming, that's something you may do exceptionally well. Fearless and wise, eagles mate for life, so fidelity is second nature to those of us who are Eagles.

When working with Indigenous people on their personal branding, I ask them to identify the cultural *and* personal strengths they bring to an organisation or workplace. This includes things like their Dreamings and totems. This fun activity is like a S.W.O.T analysis [10] but with a difference! It is an empowering activity for our mob, especially if they've never considered their unique culture and spirituality as strengths and gifts to offer the world.

Who or what has Dreaming?

Everyone and everything has Dreaming, as strange as that may sound. Crows have Dreaming. Barramundi have Dreaming. Clouds have Dreaming. To say that everyone and everything has Dreaming is to say that everything is *consciousness*. "The whole living world is informed by consciousness," says Joseph Campbell. [11] "There is a plant consciousness and there is an animal consciousness." [12] Indigenous cultures do not restrict consciousness just to living things but extend it to so-called 'inanimate' objects such as cars, crystals, rocks and stars. In Aboriginal Dreamtime, for example, even cars have Dreaming, such as the generic 'Four Wheel-drive Dreaming' or the specific 'Toyota Dreaming' while Native American people fondly refer to crystals as the Stone People, which is a lovely way of humanising them.

Steve Irwin's 'Crocodile Dreaming'

Whether you accept the idea of Dreaming is irrelevant. It is enough that our mob acknowledges and recognises it in another person. For example, it's obvious to me that the late Steve Irwin of 'Crocodile Hunter' fame clearly had Crocodile Dreaming. He was passionately drawn to these aquatic reptiles who drew him into their world. In Trevor Wie speak, Irwin's Dreaming led to his *vocation* in life.

Sometimes your personal Dreaming may not emerge from experience or insight but rather, through the epiphany of others. In Aboriginal cultures for instance, the parents or grandparents may have an experience or encounter with an animal, plant or object before a child's conception or immediately thereafter. For example, the father may go fishing and spear a fish. Later he notices a distinctive mark on his new-born not dissimilar to the mark on the fish that he speared. This affirms the child's Dreaming to him. Or the child's Dreaming (whether animal or plant) may appear in a dream with a message for the parent or grandparent. When these things happen, the prospective parents will consult a relative or Elder to confirm if they have correctly identified the child's totem. The techniques and practices vary among the nations, but the primary concepts are the same.

How does Dreamtime relate to time?

Whenever people talk about Dreamtime, they often mistakenly do so as a relic of the past. But this frozen view of history ignores its *dynamic* nature where the past, present and future are one. In the Aboriginal worldview, these events are paradoxically, happening simultaneously. Time is not linear, but a circle as symbolised by the dot. Western science has only recently come to this realisation, largely through the work of quantum physics, which has given rise to quantum computers.

Like so many of us, theoretical physicist Carlo Rovelli is also fascinated by time and has dedicated his life and career to solving its mystery. After years of research, the author of *The Order of Time* has recently concluded that ultimately, the 'mystery' of time is "more about *ourselves* than about the cosmos." [13] In this respect, his scientific thinking is more aligned with Aboriginal Dreamtime philosophy.

Others question our current reality or 'construct' and offer an alternative but intriguing view of Dreamtime.

Since its release, *The Matrix* movie has ignited debate about whether we live in a computer simulation. Before you dismiss this as some fanciful New Age theory, you should know some reputable heavyweights have lent their support to this view, including high tech entrepreneur, Elon Musk [14] and American astrophysicist Neil deGrasse Tyson [15]. Other commentators have taken it one step further in suggesting that so-called 'Dreamtime' may in fact be our *reality* rather than our present construct!

Beyond the circular nature of time, the dot reveals deeper, psychological understanding of *ourselves*, which is why it features so prominently in Aboriginal art. According to the *Book of Symbols*, the circle or dot contains everything. It is the still place where duality or opposites are reconciled - above and below, light and shade, male and female.[16] To Indigenous people, it is all of this and more. "The circle is a sacred symbol reminding us of the importance of our unique place in the universe and our relation with all things," says Native American author, Michael Garett.[17] "The more that we are able to understand the Circle of Life and our place within it, the more we are able to understand ourselves, our purpose, our responsibilities, and our Medicine." [18] Medicine, like Dreaming, refers to the spiritual *essence* within all things that can help you discover your life's purpose.

Some people fail to acknowledge the very *real* existence of Dreaming in their lives or the benefits this spirituality can offer. Not only can you discover your purpose or vocation in life but it can give you tools to cope with life. Dreamtime teaches you are *not* alone in this world - that you are more connected than you realise. That you are related to every living being - animal, plant and object. That you are *family* and that you *belong*. How incredibly empowering this realisation is to the embattled and dispossessed, and to those who have lost hope? This explains why my mentor and spiritual teacher, the late David Mowarljarlai would often remind me: "Dreamtime is not just for Aboriginal people Munya. It's for *everyone*."

What are you waiting for?

This book is my invitation to you on your Dreamtime journey.

Dreamtime Reflections

1. What is your understanding of Aboriginal Dreamtime?
2. What Dreamings do you think you might have?
3. How do your Dreamings help you cope with life?
4. Do you know which Dreaming Beings or Creative Ancestors played a key role where you were born or currently live? Who or what are they?
5. Have you ever experienced a different sense of time? What did that feel like?

Chapter 2
Laying Down The Law

Modern dancers re-enacting Dreamtime

As the Dreamtime Ancestors moved throughout the land, creating and naming everything, they laid down creation laws that are firmly fixed and immoveable. These are not so much 'laws' in the legal sense of case law, legislation and precedent. They are more in tune with Natural law, a body of unchanging moral principles doing two things. Regulating human conduct in one sense and as observable law relating to natural phenomena in another. It is in both senses that Aboriginal people refer to as 'the Law.'

Lore versus Law

Some of our mob prefer the term *lore* rather than *law* insofar as it relates to their culture. While this argument has some validity, I find it clichéd because all cultures have lore, not just us. 'Lore' is just another word for culture. It simply refers to traditional knowledge and stories about a subject that are passed down from one generation to the next. So, there is poetry lore, folklore, lore on what constitutes good manners and so on. 'Law' on the other hand specifically refers to society's rules and regulations governing human behaviour. In other words, the rights and wrongs of a culture, it's 'laws'.

Anthropologist William Stanner was especially struck by the 'ordered reality' [19] of Aboriginal Dreamtime. Everyone that plays the 'Skin Game' with me on kinship soon discover just how structured Aboriginal society is. There are strict rules and cultural protocols on all manner of things from land rights, to ceremonies and social relationships that determine who can speak for country, stories and so on. To refer to Aboriginal Dreamtime as lore therefore and not as law is to miss the entire point. It fails to acknowledge the *rule* of Aboriginal Law, of the Dreamtime Beings that created it and the Elders who police it. To refer to its rules blandly as 'lore' is to ignore the magnitude and richness of a unique ethical framework of standards informed by the Dreamtime.

Tree Law

This idea that Dreamtime Law is more in tune with *natural* law rather than legal precedent is demonstrated by the Yolngu people of Northern Territory whose symbol for their Law, *Madayin*, is a tree.[20] As with other Aboriginal nations, Yolngu maintain their law was not made by humans but as something intrinsic to the creation of the world. They see their law as having existed since the beginning of time (as laid down by the Ancestors) and having sprung from the earth itself.

Yolngu Tree Law (Madayin)

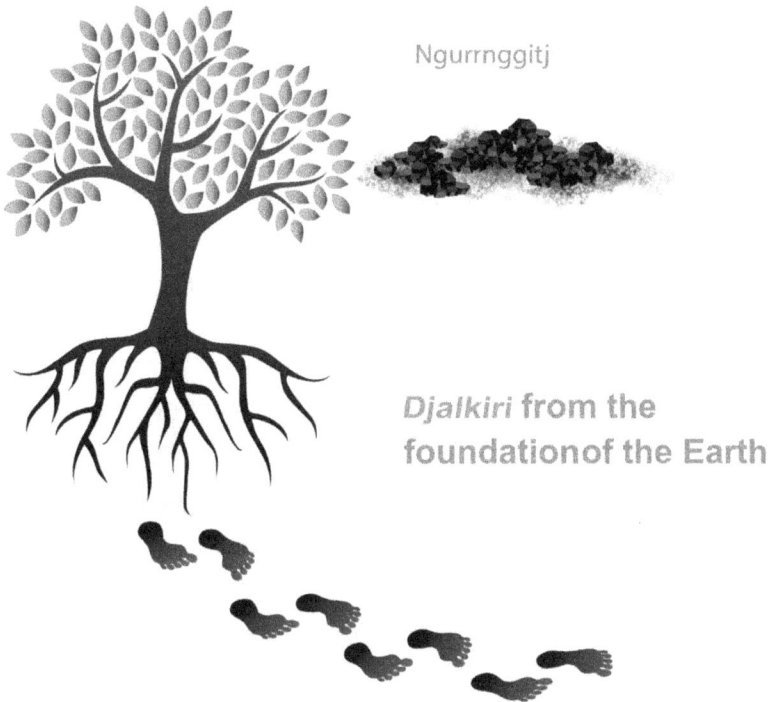

Ngurrnggitj

Djalkiri from the foundation of the Earth

The way in which Yolngu refer to their Law and the words used to describe it is revealing. Their word for Dreamtime, *Djalkirri*, means "the foot, footprint or root of a tree." [21] This is no mere linguistic mistake, for it speaks to *deeper* and profound spiritual truths. The portrayal of tree roots as footprints alludes to the early Tree Ancestors or Dreaming Beings as having *walked* over the land leaving their imprints behind. Like the Ten Commandments of the Bible that are set in stone, these footprints touch on the permanent nature of the law and attest to its *divine* creation, hence its sacredness.

This humanising of tree roots reflects the Aboriginal worldview that we are One with nature, *not* separate, and that we share a common destiny. In other words, the tree is as human as we are and vice versa.

In Yolngu culture, the tree stands for the Law and for their culture and way of life. When Yolngu explain *why* they do things in a certain way, they say it is because of the *Ngurrnggitj* or traditional practice of their people. Ngurrnggitj also refers to the overall physical structure of trees - it's leaves and roots - and its ultimate transformation from living carbon into charcoal or ash when it is burnt. Ngurrnggitj means 'charcoal or 'ashes', the leftovers of fire.[22] It hints at the life-changing powers of the Law as well as its permanence. As a Yolngu Elder explains: "When we burn the firewood, the thing that is left over when the fire burns down is the ash, and it is the same with law. It's the *real* law that lasts forever - not people's ideas and thinking." [23]

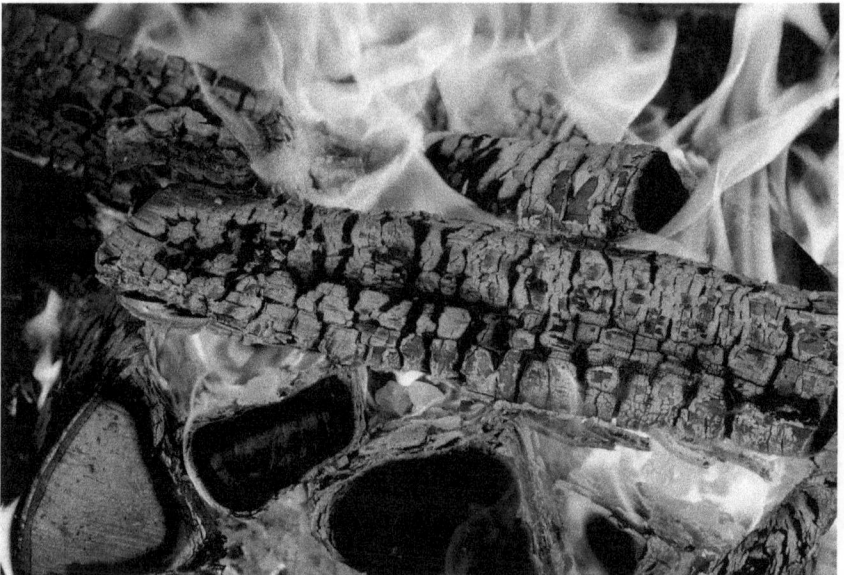

Photo Credit: Ivan Serebryannikov - Shutterstock.com

The Nurrnggitj lives on forever

My teacher, David Mowarljarlai would often talk about the permanency and non-changeable nature of Aboriginal Law. He would remind me that stories should never be changed because they are "established forever". [24] Ngurrnggitj also alludes to a tree's *shade* (*warraw*) as not only providing protection from the burning sun but as overall protection of its people. It invokes the parental powers of the Madayin as a benevolent, loving parent. "It's like all the citizens of Australia live under the shade of the Australian Government, under its care and protection. Ngurrnggitj is like a shade. We can live under its protection and care," says an Elder. [25] As the established rule of law, Ngurrnggitj determines its jurisdiction, i.e. what matters can be adjudicated upon and the extent of the power to make those decisions and judgements under the Law.

Other Law Trees

Trees feature strongly in the creation of Dreamtime Laws and in sacred teachings of other Indigenous nations, not just among Yolngu. For example, the Wandjina tribes of the Kimberley - Ngarrinyin, Worora and Wunambal tell a story of how their Law (the Wunan) was created from an ironwood tree called *Djinnang gang*. [26] Here we see another linguistic link between trees and feet as *djinna* means 'foot' in several Aboriginal languages. The story tells how a Cleverman (Law Man) split an ironwood tree in half by throwing his boomerang at it. The two split halves of the tree represent the two moieties (*Djingun* and *Wodoi*) that form the basis of kinship and marriage laws in that area. [27] What this split means in terms of kinship is explored in Chapter 7 on Skin. The choice of tool to do this is interesting because the two moieties can be represented on both ends of the boomerang (left and right), which when thrown represents an entire community in motion, the idea of moving forward together as One people.

So, what is our fascination with trees and why do they play a major role in Aboriginal spirituality? Much of the answer lies in what they symbolise. With their branches, trunk and roots, they appear almost human with features we can relate to. Like branches, our arms stretch up into the sky as we reach out to others. Our torsos mimic tree trunks while our feet approximate roots as in Yolngu Djalkirri, the tree's 'footprints'. Beyond those similarities, trees are far superior to us in many ways. It is much stronger, can stand its ground much better, lives longer and is a symbol of endurance. The tree represents what we aspire and long to be. It feeds, nourishes and sustains itself even in the worst of droughts. As if this were not enough, science now tells us that trees can talk to each other through an extensive underground network that rivals our internet and telecommunications system. What is more, trees are community-minded and care for their young. [28] And just as we have a soul, so do trees.

Burial Trees

Not surprisingly, therefore, trees play a key role in *Sorry Business* that refers to death, dying and funerals. We used to 'bury' our dead in trees before *gudia* culture imposed their burial laws on us. When a person passed, the body would be wrapped in soft bark that was painted with their clan designs that identified who they were. The soft tree bark effectively operated as the tree's outer *skin*, which is where the Aboriginal English term comes from that describes our kinship laws. The body would then be placed in trees on platforms that were built to support it. They would be left in the tree until the flesh decomposed and bones are laid bare. They would then be collected and taken away for burial in the ground or else placed somewhere special like a cave. Burial trees are called *jarrgandany* in Bardi, which translates as 'tree coffin'. We bury the dead in trees cradled in their boughs because they signify regeneration. And because they touch the underworld and the heavens, they appear to transcend space and time or the "realms of eternity." [29]

Cremation was once practised in some areas of Australia as evidenced by the skeletal remains of Mungo Lady. 'Discovered' at Lake Mungo in south-eastern Australia, her bones are believed to be at least 40,000 years old. Bones are very sacred to our people. Not only are they the physical embodiment of our loved ones but they carry their spiritual *essence* or power. Very often, gudia are drawn to Aboriginal Dreamtime seeking a deeper connection to this land. I say to them, you need not look further if the bones of your ancestors (your loved ones) are buried in this land. We do not take that lightly. For us, it is a significant and holy occurrence, for the bones of our people lie together within the body of the Rainbow Snake (regardless of our race, religion or political differences). We all return to Her in the end.

Pukumani Burial Poles

In places where tall trees are scarce, people build burial platforms or other objects instead. On the Tiwi Islands north of Darwin, burial poles are erected, ranging in height anywhere from 100cm to six foot. Carved from tree trunks, they are painted with a mixture of natural ochres and sometimes adorned with feathers and shells. Although popularly known as *Pukumani*, their actual Tiwi name is *Tutini*. [30] Pukumani means 'taboo' or 'dangerous' in the Tiwi language and is the name of their Sorry Business ceremony. It takes place two to six months after the deceased is buried. Pukumani poles were introduced to the Tiwi by their great ancestor, Purukaparli, to honour the dead. He ordered that a taboo be placed upon using the name of people who have died, which is a common Aboriginal custom. [31] Reminiscent of the famous totem poles of Native people in the Americas, Pukumani burial poles are every bit as striking and colourful, but on a smaller scale.

Pukumani Burial Poles

The Significance of Trees

Trees are sacred in many cultures and the worship of trees, in one form or another, has been practised universally around the world. Numerous stories are told about various species, including a special tree called the 'Tree of Life'. It is not so much biological as symbolic, with various species representing the sacred icon. In the Kimberley region of Western Australia, the Wandjina tribes – Ngarrinyin, Worora and Wunambal have a Tree of Life presided over by the Aboriginal goddess Jillinya.[32] Painted on a rock wall high above a waterhole called Alyaguma on the Mitchell Plateau, the sacred plum tree Golai [33] is guarded by Jillinya and several other female figures with outstretched arms and hands as if to say, 'Stop. Do not trespass'. Her dominating presence suggests all knowledge comes through her and her alone as the number one 'Boss Woman' in that area.

As with other Trees of Life, Golai teaches spiritual insight and enlightenment. Here we see the *seed language* that Robert Lawlor writes of in *Voices of the First Day* come into play. Seeds are a perfect symbol of life and death he says because "all forms of life spring from a tiny seed." [34] As they separate with leaf and root shoots, people see parallels in their own life of "dissolving the boundaries of comprehension, the self-centredness of being, the isolation of embodiment, and the fears and needs of separation." [35]

A painted footprint at the tree's base leaves no doubt it is a sacred pathway, providing moral guidance and direction to young people. Markings or segments on the tree signify the various stages of initiation. As a person progresses through the Law, they symbolically 'climb the tree' to gain ultimate spiritual mastery. A little way up the base a forked branch juts out from the right-hand side that represents *Wunan*, the kinship and sharing laws of the Kimberley, a constant reminder of our kinship obligations to each other as we journey through life. Blood-letting plays an important role in Aboriginal initiation ceremonies. Their connection to the Tree of Life is interesting given Carl Jung's comparison of trees and the human circulation system. The master of symbology noted how tree sap imitates blood as it flows down to its roots in winter before returning as fruit during the summer, thereby revealing "the entire mystery of life and death." [36]

On the east coast of Australia, the native fig tree is especially significant to the Dunghutti people who believe the souls of the dead enter it before being released into eternal Dreamtime. Several years ago, I performed a one-woman play at a hospice in Kempsey and was shown around the grounds before being taken to the Dying Room. A local fig was painted on the ceiling so that people who are dying can see their sacred tree. It was a truly moving experience, one I'll not forget.

'Inside' versus 'outside' Knowledge

There is another tree image that plays an important part in teaching Dreamtime wisdom regarding the various layers of knowledge one is entitled to. We saw earlier that there are certain restrictions based on age, clan membership and gender for example. Some individuals struggle to understand, and are even critical of, why knowledge is heavily guarded by our mob and why there are so many restrictions. What they don't realise is many other cultures in the world have spiritual 'secrets' that need to be protected. You need only look at the existence of so-called secret societies and their spiritual teachings to know this is true. The simple fact is that Aboriginal culture has high regard for the wisdom of Elders whose life experience is highly valued and respected. While younger people are spiritual beings who can offer new insights, it takes a lifetime to become an adept. Just ask any bishop, rabbi or imam. Aboriginal Elders achieve spiritual mastery over a lifetime of learning before passing this on to younger people through initiation and character trials to determine whether a person is worthy of it. As elitist as that may sound, it is borne out of human experience, tried and tested over thousands of years. As we know, with great knowledge comes even greater responsibility.

This sensitivity around protecting sacred information is not only an Aboriginal concern. Even Jesus Christ talks about this in his famous 'Sermon on the Mount' when he exhorted his followers, "Do not cast your pearls before swine" (Matthew 7:6). Intrigued by this biblical passage, I have long pondered its true meaning. A common interpretation is that you should not offer or show something valuable, good, or beautiful to someone who does not understand its value or appreciate it. But I think Christ was saying much *more* than this. I think he is warning against the potential misuse or abuse of spiritual knowledge and powers for personal gain or sinister reasons. In this regard, he is closely aligned with Aboriginal Elders who zealously guard Dreamtime secrets to prevent this abuse. While a Dreamtime secrecy code exists, it is there to ensure against individual manipulation, an issue that all religions must grapple with.

You may recall my friend Trevor Wie who I introduced you to in the first chapter. An example that he gives of Elders protecting Dreamtime information is where they only ever pass on 'children's stories' to the Australian public. This is largely because of the disrespect shown to Aboriginal people and their culture says Trevor. "You know... they stopped telling European mob stuff when they were getting slaughtered and they said, 'Well there's no respect,' so we just tell 'em the children's level or public level story." [37] Not knowing the full story effectively means people miss out on the wondrous *gems* contained in them. This is truly sad, for just like all the other great religious traditions, Dreamtime has much to offer humanity by way of spiritual guidance, solace and wisdom. This practice of our mob withholding sacred information by only sharing *children's* stories with the Australian public touches upon an important teaching.

When accessing Dreamtime wisdom, our people distinguish between *inside* and *outside* knowledge. They point to the outer and inner parts of a tree, namely the bark and the inner heartwood, to demonstrate this. The bark is the tree's skin, soft and malleable, versus the inside wood that is solid and of greater substance. The bark represents outer knowledge, as in *children's* stories, versus the inner or deeper knowledge contained in adult stories that are symbolised by the heartwood. Sociologist Emile Durkheim first referred to this division in terms of the 'sacred and profane' in *The Elementary Forms of the Religious Life.* Or put simply, that which is holy and that which is not.

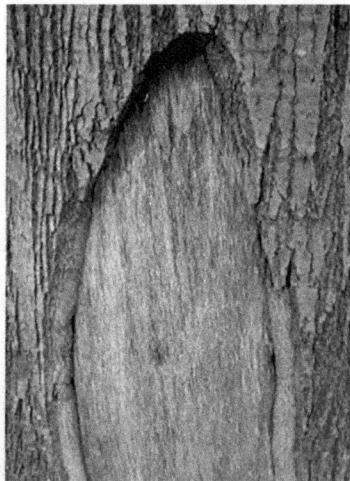

Outside = bark
Profane

Inside = wood
Sacred

Inner and Outer Dreamtime Knowledge

Another way of 'reading' this symbol is to follow Joseph Campbell's advice. There is no separation between nature and ourselves, he says, and when we don't make that connection, we "misread the image." [38] So, this notion of 'inside' and 'outside' knowledge is not so much never the twain shall meet, quite the opposite really. "The inner world," says Campbell, "is the world of your requirements and your energies and your structure and your possibilities that meets the outer world. And the outer world is the field of your incarnation. That's where you are. You've got to keep both going." [39] Quoting Novalis, he reminds us that "The seat of the soul is there where the inner and outer worlds meet." [40] Dreamtime unites these two worlds and takes us there to the seat of the soul.

Scar Trees

Scattered throughout the Australian continent are numerous *scar trees*. The scars are created from making canoes, shields and other weapons, and they differ in depth and size. Ever mindful of our 'carbon footprint', we only take what we need from the land. Rather than fell a whole tree to make one object, we cut out what is needed rather than destroy it entirely. Mimicking the human body, the tree creates a scar to cover its 'wound'. Scar trees are either marked or unmarked. The marked ones are engraved and decorated with special symbols. The plain ones are used to make canoes, coolamons and shields. The engraved trees are holy because they mark places of special significance such as a sacred site or place of initiation and are used as spiritual teaching aids. They also show the difference between *inside/outside* knowledge. When Aboriginal men and women are initiated into the sacred mysteries, they cut their bodies to mark their transition. Like Maori *moko* (tattoos), initiation scars are worn as a badge of pride that signals to others that they have 'gone through the Law'. Places where these law ceremonies are held imbue the land with powerful energies that make them holy.

Aboriginal Scar Tree with Sacred Symbols

During the initiation ceremony, ash and clay are inserted into the initiate's wounds, forming huge welts called cicatrices. This means they carry the Dreaming of the Earth inside their bodies to remind them of their connection to the land. Like Christians, we are reminded of our Earthly origins as in the funeral prayer, "Ashes to ashes, dust to dust and to dust you shall return." (Genesis 3:19) Aboriginal people know that when we die, we return to Mother Earth, the Snake and to the eternal Dreamtime. The carved symbols on Scar Trees echo human initiation scars and vice versa.

Scar Clan and Sacred Scars

In *Women Who Run With The Wolves*, Clarissa Pinkola Estes tells how stories contain healing medicine. In her chapter on 'Scar Clan,' she talks about the special gifts that scarring brings to those who have suffered in some unjust way. [41] Like Aboriginal people who wear their initiation scars with pride, Scar Clan members are reminded of the pain they have endured in life and how they have survived to emerge stronger, wiser and more compassionate. She encourages women not to count their ages in years but by their "battle scars". When people ask her how old she is, she replies "I am *seventeen* battle scars old." So, when you are asked your ethnicity or nationality, she exhorts, "smile enigmatically and say, Scar Clan." [42] After all, you've earned it!

As someone who loves languages - their origin and the meaning of words - I am a huge fan of word play to illustrate spiritual concepts that feature in my teachings. When I look at the word *sacred* for example, I see several things that tell me how special it is. The first thing I see is the colour *red* as celebrated in red ochre, which is *the* primary colour of Aboriginal Law Business. Red symbolises blood the life force, which is why it is sacred. Then there is the *Red Sac* or the way of the heart (Red Sac is *sacred* backwards). I also see the words *scar* and *scared*. Scars speak to initiation and to be scared is to be in awe of something greater than ourselves. So, being scarred is another way of saying you're *scared*, which is all about having respect for something greater than us.

When I lived in Lismore, New South Wales in the late 90's, my friend's house caught fire. When I walked in to the burnt house to have a look, I was completely overwhelmed by the presence of Kali, the Hindu goddess of destruction. In that blackened room, I experienced an extraordinary sense of awe and reverence for her that left me shaken to the core. I now understand how the Quakers received their moniker. It was like walking into a sacred temple. I felt incredibly humbled before the Black One who gifted me with her presence. I now have the deepest feelings of reverence for Her.

Acknowledging sacredness is about respecting a Higher Power. Indigenous people know that *fear* is an important but normal part of spiritual learning. Individuals become brave through activities such as spending nights alone in the bush as a necessary part of their initiation. After you have confronted your fear of the dark and night terrors, you emerge a spiritual warrior unafraid of nothing and no-one.

Dreamtime Reflections

1. What is your understanding of Aboriginal law? How does it differ from the western legal system?
2. Can you think of other ways that trees are significant in our lives? Do you have a special tree that you relate to? How is it special to you?
3. If you follow a specific religion or spiritual tradition, can you identify an example of what may be considered as inside versus outside knowledge?
4. Do you have any scars, tattoos or piercings? Do they hold any significance to you? Are they a painful or positive reminder?
5. Have you ever experienced a deep sense of awe and reverence for someone or something?

Chapter 3
Songlines

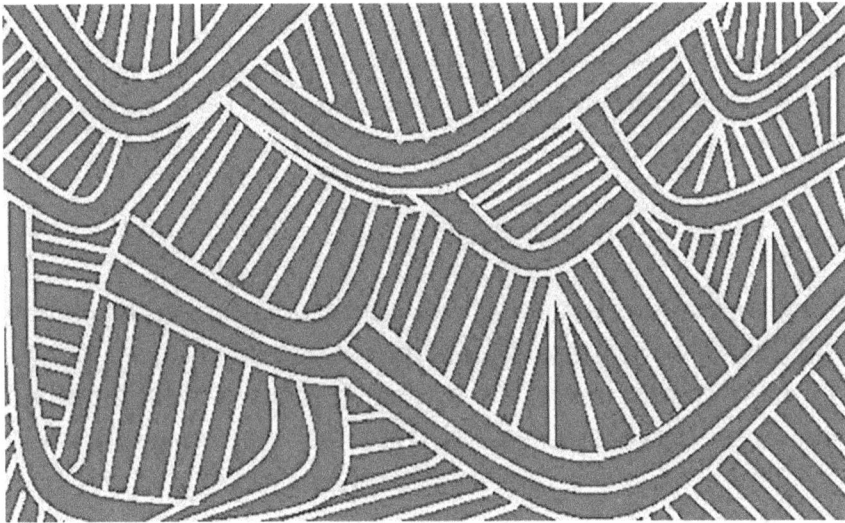

Wunan by Munya Andrews

Songlines or 'Dreaming Tracks' as they are also known, are energy lines that criss-cross the Australian continent. Together they form a net that holds everything together as in the Kimberley concept of the Wunan. Popularised by Bruce Chatwin in 1989, *Songlines* mark the routes followed by Dreaming Beings during the creative era of the Dreamtime as recorded in traditional dances, songs, stories and paintings. [43] Travelling across the land and sky, the ancestors named everything in their wake, leaving behind their *footprints* in the form of marks or scratches on the land. When their job was complete, some of these beings returned to the heavens from where they came while others turned into stone where they can still be seen today in the landscape. Some beings walked through rock walls as portals into another dimension, leaving their imprint behind like photographic memories. These 'photos' were painted over by Aboriginal people, resulting in cave or rock paintings. Each year they are repainted by senior law men and women in ceremonial rituals as they are being sung. Songs and stories re-tell the heroic deeds of these sacred beings and are used to instruct young people in Dreamtime Law. Therefore, no individual will claim authorship of these paintings. Instead, they maintain they were there from the Dreamtime.

Virtual star maps and other guides

Songlines are virtual maps in our heads and a navigation tool just like the stars. As people retrace steps taken by the ancestral creator beings and by singing songs in the appropriate sequence, they can easily navigate vast distances regardless of whether they are familiar with their immediate surrounds or not. Songs describe the land's geological features such as billabongs, creeks, hills, mountains, rivers and waterholes. Bush foods are recorded in detail that tell the singer where certain foods are and when they are available. More than just navigational aids, songlines are survival tools. With a plentiful supply of food and water, a traveller can survive the harshest of environments.

Aboriginal people learn these maps through songs and stories, but not everyone has immediate access to them. They are closely guarded secrets, which one must be initiated into. Various factors come into play that determine whether an individual is entitled to the entire Dreaming cycle or to specific segments only. Such factors include, age, gender and what clan someone belongs to. This means that not everyone has the full songline sequence in their head. It may be that only a part of the song or story is known and therefore only a part of the total map. Only a Cleverman or Cleverwoman will know a songline in its entirety. This knowledge is gained through a lifetime of learning marked by various stages of initiation where pieces or segments of the songline are revealed.

Songlines that follow the path of celestial Dreaming Beings as they travel through Sky Country provide a virtual map of the stars. They also serve as calendars depicting the seasons. Even though these star maps feature the cardinal directions - north, south, east and west, the seasons are not limited to four as in western society. Like Native Americans and other Indigenous people, Indigenous calendars go beyond the proverbial four seasons. Some calendars have as many as six, eight or more seasons.

A vast network of songlines

Given the rich diversity of Aboriginal nations, not surprisingly, there is an extensive system of songlines that stretch throughout the Australian continent. While some are just a few kilometres, others cover vast distances, hundreds of kilometres long. Each one follow routes of the creator beings and so flow in a certain direction, either from east to west or north to south and vice versa. Some of the better known songlines are that of Sun Woman and Moon Man, *Wati Kutjarra* or 'Two Men', *Magara* the 'Seven Sisters', Dingo Dreaming and most significant of all - that of the Rainbow Snake. Songlines follow set directions so that walking the wrong way along a songline may be considered a sacrilegious act. Since a songline can span the lands of several nations, parts of the song may be sung in different languages altogether. Despite this, language is not a barrier because the melody of the song describes the contour of the land over which the song passes. So even if someone doesn't know the local name for a physical feature such as a hill or valley, they can intuit it from the song's rhythm. The rhythm is crucial to understanding the song. Listening to the song of the land is the same as walking on this songline. Although many songlines have been lost in places where colonisation has had a devastating impact, it may be possible to reconstruct.

I once did a creative, revealing exercise mapping a Wathurong songline by following the Yarra River using Koori place names of suburbs, streets and roads. I was startled to discover they perfectly matched the land they described. This is a fun activity you can do yourself through research and a curious mind. Or else you could trace your surrounding environment and with each twist and turn, each nuance, compose a song that celebrates the land and your place in it.

Some songlines extend out to sea where people have country under the ocean, such as my Bardi people. These stretches of submerged land also have sacred sites that tell stories of oceanic Ancestors who travelled through the islands they created, including reefs, sandbanks and marine creatures. These Dreaming Beings named all the places in Bardi-Jawi sea country.[44] Along the way, they performed special ceremonies where they left ritual paraphernalia behind that turned into reef and rock on the sea bed. Their adventures are recalled in songs and stories. Bardi knowledge of their marine ecosystems is considerable. There is deep understanding of the tides, times when seafood is available, and characteristics of species being hunted. This environmental expertise is reflected in our six-season calendar. *Gulil* the turtle, is a much loved and sought-after food item and plays a pivotal role in Bardi spirituality. *Lalin* marks the season known as 'Married Turtle' time when ceremonies commence in October through to December, to *Ungulgul,* from the end of December through to January when

Married Turtle season ends. These seasons refer to Married Turtles because this is the time when they are mating and are found floating on the water, which makes it easy to catch them. When we say, 'I love you' in Bardi it is usually said in full sentence, 'Ny lian narmanju ardijan arngrimin gulil' (I love you until there are no more baby turtles). The turtle's demise signalling the end of marriage or a romantic relationship.

Married Turtles season Lalin - Ungulgul

The *country* someone comes from plays a key role in their cultural and social identity. People who live along the coast and offshore islands, for instance, will refer to themselves as *saltwater* people as opposed to *freshwater* or *riverside* tribes and *desert* people. Their Dreamings will reflect the environment on which their traditional lands are located. For example, saltwater people are likely to have Dreamings based on marine creatures such as dolphins, dugongs, saltwater crocodiles and turtles whereas freshwater people, riverside tribes or desert people will not. Their Dreamings will feature land-based animals and plants only found in those environments such as dingo, emu, kangaroo and so on.

In Torres Strait Islander communities of northern Australia, the dugong or sea cow is one of their most revered deities whose songline documents the travels of their marine Ancestor from the west to the eastern islands. The first time I flew to *Mer* (Murray Island), I was greeted by a white dugong and her calf in the waters below my plane. I told a local Torres Strait Islander leader, Jim Akee, what I saw, and he told me that was a special gift welcoming me to the islands, a rare sight not seen by everyone. I felt enormously privileged that their Ancestors had trusted and bestowed such a gift to me.

Yorro Yorro - Singing the Land

Aboriginal people believe the land must be continually sung to keep it 'alive'. Singing the land is tied up with the propagation and renewal of animal and plant species, including humans. It is closely aligned with *love magic*. As one female Elder remarked, "We don't just sing for *jardada* (love magic) but for country." [45] Among the Wandjina tribes of the Kimberley - the Ngarrinyin, Worora and Wunambal, singing the land is called *Yorro Yorro*, which effectively means "everything standing up alive". [46] This ongoing creation and renewal of life lies embedded in the land, which is why *connection to country* is so important. These songs, as we have seen, are musical stories of the journeys of spirit ancestors during the Dreamtime. They vary in length and duration from short through to epic song cycles that may take days to recite. Even though people faithfully follow scripts laid down long ago during the Dreamtime, there is room for creativity. For example, sometimes a new song will be 'found' in a dream and may become part of existing songlines and networks. This happens more frequently with an Elder rather than a younger or uninitiated person. Having said that, anyone can sing the land, not just Aboriginal people.

In my Dreamtime workshops, I teach traditional songs but also encourage people to compose their own. Several years ago, I ran a special Dreamtime workshop just for women on my friend Maria Eleni Alesandra's property in Hall, New South Wales near Canberra. Besides singing the land, we did Love Magic. Some two weeks later I received a telephone call from her enquiring, "Munya, what did we *do*?" In reply, I asked, "What do you mean?" Maria Eleni excitedly told me there was an article in *The Canberra Times* which reported that local scientists were baffled by the return of a bird species previously thought to be extinct! I explained to her that the whole purpose of singing the land is to create supply of plants and animals, known as 'increase rituals'. She was astounded and said, "If we can do that by singing the land, imagine what the *cockies* (farmers) of Australia could achieve if they all sang the country!"

Singing the land is about maintaining harmony and balance to ensure the fertility of the land so that it can feed and nourish us. It also enables us to commune with the land and the spiritworld. Dancing, as we know, creates altered states of consciousness but so does singing, as evidenced by religious chants designed to create meditative states. The combination of these two powerful forces is formidable. When Aboriginal people dance and sing their stories, they take on characteristics of the ancestral beings they are portraying in the ceremonies. Some dancers mimic these beings like Kangaroo Man so well that they appear as actual kangaroos, such that the line between human and animal becomes blurred, indistinguishable from each other. Audiences think, "Oh it's because they're so in tune with nature." But it is so much *more* than that. By mimicking animals, they become in tune with the Oneness that pervades all things. By dancing and behaving as that animal, they align themselves to its essence and our kindredness.

It is in this sense that people at Yarralin in the Northern Territory proudly proclaim *Dingo Makes Us Human* as in the book by Deborah Bird Rose. Like the Rainbow Snake, Dingo plays a pivotal role in Aboriginal spirituality. Also called Dog Dreaming, there are significant Dingo Dreaming songlines running across the Australian continent, from east to west from Queensland to Western Australia and north to south down through the interior. Red ochre associated with this Dreaming is referred to as the 'Blood of the Dog'. When I asked an Elder about the significance of Dingo Dreaming, she replied, "Munya, what does *dog* spell backwards?"

Dadirri (Deep Listening)

An important part of communicating with the land is knowing how to listen to it, as we believe that country speaks to us. We are taught from a tender age how to do this. Just as we communicate with each other, we are taught the importance of listening with our heart, mind and soul. In my Dreamtime workshops, I teach people how to develop what I call, *Dreaming Ears* and *Dreaming Eyes*. It reminds me of Christ's teachings where he refers to "he who has ears to hear". (Matthew 11:15 and Mark 4:9, 23). This passage contrasts types of hearers - those who do not take notice of the Word of God and those who truly listen and seek understanding. Dreamtime is no different to Christianity or any of the other great religions that seek to understand our place in the world, for our lives to have meaning and connection. It matters not how you get there, whether it is through Jesus, Muhammad or the Rainbow Snake.

All Indigenous nations of Australia have their own version and understanding of the practice of dadirri or 'deep listening'.

The dadirri version comes from the Northern Territory made famous by Aboriginal Elder, Aunty Miriam Rose Ungunmerr-Baumann. Dadirri is a meditation practice that teaches people how to connect with the land and each other through sacred breathing. It is about tuning oneself to the cycles and rhythms of life. As Aunty Miriam Rose reminds us:

We are River People
We cannot hurry the river
We need to move with the current and understand its ways. [47]

To 'move with the current and understand its ways' is to enter the Dreamtime, to connect with its rhythms and move at a different pace to what you are accustomed to, especially in our modern hectic lifestyle. Dadirri reminds us to 'Stop and smell the roses'. To understand the ways of the river is to step outside and leave your ego behind because it is *not* all about you. It is about learning your place in the world, to see beauty in everything around you and to cultivate acceptance – accepting that the world moves according to its own pace, as do people. "Understanding the flow of life allows us to let go of expectations, accept the limitations over which we have no control, and move with this flow," says Native American author, Michael Garrett. [48]

Not just important for spiritual reasons, "Listening is an overlooked leadership tool," in the business world says Melissa Daimler. [49] When done well, she says, listening creates safety in the workplace. A difficult skill to master, she has identified three types of listening. The first of these is *internal* listening where you focus on your own "thoughts, worries and insecurities". [50] The second kind is *focused* listening where you concentrate on the other person but may miss out on the nuances of communication. The final kind is *360* (degrees) listening. "This is where the *magic* happens," says Daimler. [51] This kind of listening focuses on energies and connection with another person where you not only listen to what they're saying but *how* they're saying it and "even better, what they're *not* saying." [52] This 360-degree listening is the same as Dadirri and other Indigenous ways of listening. It is listening with the heart as well as the ears.

Dreaming Ears and Dreaming Eyes

As we learn to open our ears to listen to the land, we are also taught to open our eyes to observe it carefully. This means taking notice of *signs* however small. While it helps to have keen eyesight, we are also taught to see with our third eye. Here we begin to enter the psychic realm of the shaman or *mabarn*. The extraordinary psychic abilities of the Cleverman or Cleverwoman are well documented. While western society calls these abilities *extra* sensory perception or ESP, to our people, they are a part of *normal* life. We believe the spiritworld is part of this material one. There is no separation, but Oneness. Dreamtime speaks to that Oneness of creation to its splendour and glory.

The celebrated psychoanalyst, Carl Jung shared an experience he had that demonstrates this feeling of Oneness. In *Memories, Dreams and Reflections*, he tells how he would often sit on a large stone in his backyard to meditate and relax. One day, he thought deeply about the relationship he had with this rock and pondered, "Am I the one who is sitting on the stone, or am I the stone on which he is sitting?" [53] Perplexed by this question it was never made clear to him but he says, "there was no doubt whatsoever that this stone stood in some secret relationship with me." [54] What Jung experienced and felt is what many Aboriginal people think and feel in relation to their country and the world around them. We would say that he was touched by the Dreamtime.

'I am sitting on top of this stone and it is underneath. Am I the one who is sitting on the stone or am I the stone on which he is sitting?'

Carl Jung

What other people regard as mere superstition, we see as messages from the spiritworld. We are always looking for signs that tell us things; sometimes a warning or a message from loved ones. Things like a perfectly healthy tree falling in the bush for no explicable reason will catch our attention as being spiritually significant. Many other Aboriginal people have shared similar stories with me, countless times.

People ask, "Munya, how can I develop Dreaming Eyes?"

A simple way is to choose a section of the land to focus on. It could be a rock formation like Rosette Rock at Organ Pipes National Park, a small creek or a tree. Just focus on that one item and allow your mind to wander. If the image is powerful enough, you will start to feel it drawing you into its portal. Don't fight the feeling. Allow it to take you where it will. If you find it hard to focus or nothing is happening, let your eyes wander freely. This is what I do to see those Magic Pictures that have an underlying image. When asked how to see them, I tell people to look *behind* the image. The same principle applies here. Try it. You may just be amazed at what you see and experience.

With Dreaming Eyes, you begin to see human and animal faces in everything - clouds, mountains and trees. Apparently, seeing faces in inanimate objects is quite common, and has a name - pareidolia. It's described as a 'psychological' phenomenon, but to Aboriginal people, this is *spiritual* and very real. My dear friend and teacher, the late Aunty Lorraine Mafi-Williams, a Bundjalung Elder of the Gittabul clan in Lismore, New South Wales, saw these faces as *spirits*. A film maker, she incorporated an image of an Aboriginal female spirit in a tree in her documentary on Dreamtime to demonstrate this principle.

Pareidolia is believed to be the human brain lending significance and facial features to 'random' patterns. I see faces all the time wherever I travel, and not just in Australia. These patterns are not random to me, far from it. They are *real* images that tell me something of the Dreaming of Place. They show me the ancestry of place - which groups of people have passed through the land throughout history - and the results are nothing short of amazing. I have seen Maori faces in Aotearoa and Native American faces in America. At other times, I have seen a mixture of ethnic faces in places you'd least expect that isn't supported by official versions of history. This tells me more about humanity's travels than any history book.

Scientists also say pareidolia is part of evolution – that our survival depended on seeing faces of animals that threatened our survival. However, I would explain this phenomenon from a Dreamtime perspective. To me, seeing faces in the land is acknowledging *Spirit*, our common heritage and destiny, our connection, our kindredness and our Oneness with all of nature. The truth is that we are more connected than we realise - that we are not alone in this world but part of one big family. As human beings, the pinnacle of our existence is to realise our *true* spiritual nature - to become One with ourselves, with each other, to all living creatures and the world in which we live. Surely this is the primary objective of all religions. Dreamtime is a pathway to achieving that.

Dreamtime Reflections

1. Can you see instances where Songlines might apply in your life?
2. Try writing a poem or a song that celebrates land that has special meaning to you. It could be where you were born or where you live today.
3. Try practising dadirri or deep listening the next time you go walking in the bush. Take notice of your surroundings and pay deep attention. Do you notice anything different? Are sounds the same? What is the land saying to you?
4. Have you ever had an experience like Carl Jung sitting on a rock? What did you discover about yourself?
5. Do you see images in the landscape? Are they animals, people or something else?

Chapter 4
Sacred Sites

Kakadu National Park

Aboriginal sacred sites are a contentious political issue in Australia, largely because of the cultural clashes that involve mining and other land development projects. Our people have been wrongly accused of fabricating stories about sacred sites to halt these initiatives, with disastrous consequences for everyone. The Hindmarsh Island (*Kumarangk*) fiasco [55] is a perfect example of this. There are many others. What these cases reveal is not only a clash of cultural values but a total lack of understanding and respect of Aboriginal religious beliefs and practices. This chapter is an attempt to provide some basic understanding of what sacred sites *are* and why they are so important to our spiritual well-being.

I'm often asked: If all land is sacred to Aboriginal people, how is it that there are sacred 'sites'? Isn't this a contradiction? The term can be misleading because it implies that only a specific territorial tract of land is special as opposed to the entire continent. A more useful way to think about sacred sites is as *places of power*. These are places where the ancestral earth energies are highly concentrated at a certain spot that has spiritual meaning or associations connected to a Dreamtime story. As you travel along a songline, you will inevitably encounter these special places where a certain event occurred involving a creator. It may be where a dance or song was created or where some other significant event transpired. As part of the act of creation, a creator will leave behind energetic residue at that location. This is what is commonly referred to as the *Dreaming* of that place. In concentrated form this residue is so powerful it can overwhelm and disorient a person, especially if they are uninitiated in law from that area. And because sites are categorised according to gender, someone of the wrong sex approaching it may be spiritually and psychologically affected because they have ignored cultural protocols.

A young man from Noonkanbah in the Kimberley told me a story of the land changing its appearance before his very eyes so that he got lost. His explanation for losing his way was couched in spiritual terms of country having the power to do this. According to my teacher, David Mowarljarlai our *gi* (spirit) pushes us back. [56] He says, "If you don't have enough energy to concentrate, it pushes you back, can make you confused, even changing the painting or the area so it can't be recognised." [57] Some Aboriginal people are afraid of the bush for these reasons. Ultimately there is nothing to be afraid of as my teacher, David Mowarljarlai would often say, "Munya, the bush *gives* us power." This explains why you feel so refreshed and rejuvenated there. You may think you are going on a bush walk but you are doing much more than that - you are walking in the footsteps of our Ancestors for they are *your* Ancestors too, not just mine.

Cultural protocols for sacred sites

There are a few basic protocols you need to be aware of. When I lived on Bundjalung country in northern New South Wales in the early 2000's with my mentor and teacher, Aunty Lorraine Mafi-Williams, she shared a story of Nimbin Rocks. An Aboriginal Elder, she was approached by a group of white women who were worried about the high number of miscarriages suffered by women living close to them. Aunty Lorraine explained this was happening because Nimbin Rocks is a men's site which women are not supposed to visit. When they became aware of this, they moved away from its immediate proximity resulting in successfully carrying their babies to full-term and it no longer became an issue. This is not just a male thing. Men are not allowed to visit women's areas either. This is to give space to men and women to do their own thing, and allow each other to just be.

I experienced the spiritual consequence for inadvertently doing the wrong thing. At Barwon Heads in Victoria, I made the mistake of walking in the direction of the high red cliff that juts out into the Southern Ocean. Normally I check with my *lian* (spirit) to see if I have permission to be there as it warns me to not go where I'm not supposed to. I must have missed the signs because the next morning I experienced a mild form of paralysis upon waking and could not get out of bed. Instead of thinking something was wrong with me in a medical sense, I immediately sought a cultural explanation. I instinctively knew that my predicament was the result of doing the 'wrong' thing. So, in my mind I retraced my steps of where I had gone the previous day and like a flash of lightning, it came to me. I had walked where I should not have walked! There was no way of knowing for sure, but it was probably because that area was men's business. Once I realised my error, I apologised profusely to the Old People (spirits). Once I did that my paralysis disappeared, and I was free to get up and walk. Other Aboriginal people have shared stories with me of becoming similarly incapacitated or else totally disoriented in space and time such that they were unable to find their way in the bush. Cultural explanations are usually given to rationalise these situations.

Love Magic and Conception sites

As the creator beings moved throughout the land, they deposited the spirits of unborn children or *rai* along the way. Many of these places are regarded as fertility sites that enable a woman to become pregnant if she so desires. Australian actress Nicole Kidman famously credited the 'fertility waters' surrounding Kununurra in Australia's north west for helping her conceive after years of desperately trying. This allegedly occurred during the filming of Baz Luhrmann's *Australia* movie starring Kidman. Released in 2008, it co-starred Hugh Jackman and David Wenham. [58]

Fertility Waters of Kununurra

In addition to visiting fertility sites such as the one above, conception can also be aided through *jarada* or love magic. Presided over by Aboriginal goddesses Gudgeri and Gunabibi, love magic is 'women's business'. The routes taken by these female ancestors, form love magic songlines whose recitals aid in fertility and the manifestation of love relationships. Love Magic is a form of creative visualisation. Thought to be a product of the 'New Age,' in fact, there is nothing 'new' about it. It is an age-old technique shared by many cultures around the world. Love Magic is not just an 'increase' ritual but a reminder of our individual and collective creative powers to attract whatever we want in life.

In my Dreamtime workshops, I not only teach people how to sing for country but how to create Love Magic. We do this by singing the land as we paint small stones. River stones are better suited for their smooth surface. Their rounded edges resemble seeds or eggs from which their visions grow or are hatched. This is such a joyous activity with much laughter and frivolity. It immediately puts us in a childhood state where there are no restrictions or limitations to our imagination so we can create to our heart's content. Ask yourself, what is it you really want in life? Is it a special one-on-one, intimate, love relationship? Is it a new job? Is it world peace, inner harmony or all three? Love Magic can call that in for you if you are open to it.

What is the 'Dreaming' of Place?

Like other Indigenous people, many of our mob believe in the *unseen* world of energies, forces and spirits beyond our material, physical reality. Central to the notion of Dreaming something into existence is the concept of *jiva* or *guruwarri*. In *Voices of the First Day*, Robert Lawlor describes guruwarri as 'seed power' deposited in the earth during that first, initial act of creation. It "leaves behind a *vibrational residue* in the earth, as plants leave an image of themselves as seeds." [59] All of nature is perceived as a 'symbolic footprint' of the world's creator beings. "As with a seed, the potency of an earthly location is wedded to the memory of its origin," says Lawlor. This 'potency' is what Aboriginal people refer to as the 'Dreaming' of a place. It is only "in extraordinary states of consciousness can one be aware of, or attuned to, the inner dreaming of the earth." [60] These 'extraordinary' states of consciousness that Lawlor refers to are largely achieved through ritual and meditation involving the use of special herbs, chants, dance, music and songs.

The 'initial acts of creation' are not things that happened in the 'past,' for time is not linear in Aboriginal philosophy. Rather, the perception of time as being one means the 'past' is accessible today. The Observer Effect in quantum physics is relevant here. This theory acknowledges that simply observing a situation or phenomenon necessarily changes that event.

The inclusion of people as 'observers' in this equation beyond instrumentation has led to the popular belief that a conscious mind can directly affect reality. [61] What this means effectively, is that we all get to play an active role in creation, which is incredibly empowering. Aboriginal people engage in this co-creation process each time they *sing* the land as in *Yorro Yorro* where everything stands up.

Sacred sites are places of spiritual insight

As a huge fan of word play, I encourage people to consider the hidden meaning of language to get to its true essence. For example, *site* can also refer to things that we *see* as in our *sight*. So, a sacred site then becomes sacred sight or the place of our 'in site' or *insight*. These are places of huge personal and divine revelation, which is why people seek them out. Anyone who has ever visited a sacred site intuitively understands this. Sacred sites are the *locus* and sacred sights become the *opus*. In other words, spiritual insight is gained not only through what we can see (as in 'optics') but what we can visit and touch (as in 'locus' or place).

People who visit Uluru in central Australia often comment on its other-worldly presence, saying how much it feels like a sacred cathedral or temple even though it is not a man-made structure. When I first visited the Red Rock in 1985, I was struck by its majestic, spiritual presence. As I approached from afar, it slowly grew in stature, appearing on the horizon almost in a dreamlike state. The air was full of expectation as the stone sentinel silently sat waiting, watching and breathing. I have felt the same sense of reverence at other sacred places, from the Organ Pipes in Victoria, to Devils Tower in Wyoming, to Stonehenge in England. Always I am deeply moved, enriched and empowered after visiting them.

Sacred pilgrimage

The idea of re-enacting the travels of spirit ancestors along songlines is akin to undertaking a pilgrimage. A pilgrimage is a journey, especially a long one, made to a sacred place as an act of religious devotion. My teacher, David Mowarljarlai, would often say to me, "Munya, it's important to remember that Wandjina *walked* everywhere." Walking is a form of meditation that creates a relaxed state. But when we walk on the land, we are doing much *more* than that. We are following in the footsteps of our Ancestors. This is a sacred and profound act. By walking in their footsteps, singing the songs, recounting their deeds through dance and story, we connect and commune with that spirit ancestor. Not only do we become one with them but in so doing, are gifted with spiritual insight and wisdom beyond our wildest imagination.

We are taught from a young age to walk barefoot on the land because knowledge contained within it passes through the *souls* of our feet. (The word play here is intentional). The realisation of this teaching is incredibly empowering to the Stolen Generation; Aboriginal people removed from their families as part of Australian government policy. They sometimes feel that because because of their experience that they have that they have somehow 'lost' their culture. But I say to them, "You haven't lost anything Bub. It is all there in the land that you *belong* to and are a part of. You come from the Dreamtime and you are a force to be reckoned with. You may feel you are alone but you have a long line of Ancestors standing beside you, guiding and protecting you. Go in peace and claim your birth right." I encourage people to take off their shoes in the bush and walk barefoot on the land to commune with it but with the proviso not to do this on Snake Country for obvious reasons!

Walking on Sacred Land

When Aboriginal people walk in the bush, it is with purpose and intent. There is no walking just for the sake of recreation. When they walk, they are focused, attentive and prepared in every sense; mentally, physically and spiritually. It's important to concentrate on your environment and be aware to not only avoid danger but to be fully conversant with it. Gudia tend to walk with their eyes fixed on the horizon, paying scant attention to their immediate surrounds. By not looking down, you can miss an entire ecosystem at your feet and a multitude of signs.

The *gudia* way of walking is also a metaphor for life where you become transfixed on the future, ignoring the past and the present. By forever searching for or looking at what lies ahead beyond the horizon makes it difficult to remain in the *now*. While Aboriginal people are aware of what lies ahead, they are more interested in the peripheral. This makes it easier to focus and concentrate on one's surrounds, rather than become distracted. You can never get lost in the bush if you walk in this way for your brain will recall everything. When we listen deeply to our *lian* or *gi* (spirit) we are guided and protected always. You cannot get lost when you listen to your inner voice and when you listen to the land that speaks to us. As my teacher, David Mowarljarlai explains: "When your mind is tuned in and directed towards your gi symbol, you are in an ancient state of mind; time stands still, because your mind is in a state where time does not count. It's not like dreaming, seeing things in your sleep. Ancient time is no time." [62] To go back in time, you walk. It gives you respect for what happened when everything was created. It gives you a quietness of mind and direction. Try it and see how it feels.

We saw earlier that *all* the land is sacred because the land is our mother. Just like a mother, she nourishes and sustains us. It will come as no surprise therefore that several words for land are also the root words to describe a pregnant woman, such as *boodjaree* in the Noongar language and *boogajin* in Nyul Nyul. *Boodja* and *buru* are respective terms for 'land' in their tongues. And so, when we walk on the land, we not only follow the footsteps of our Ancestors but we walk on our Mother. Therefore, we do so respectfully. This means walking *gently* on the land - not stomping through with heavy boots, making loud noises or carrying ghetto blasters. In my Dreamtime courses, I teach people how to walk respectfully on the land in silence with much reverence, listening deeply with our *Dreaming Ears* and observing with our *Dreaming Eyes*. One of the first things they learn to do is announce their presence. The way to do this varies among the nations, but a common practice is to throw pebbles in front of you to alert the Old People (spirits) that you are coming towards them. The pebbles are like a knock on the door that lets them know you are about to enter. The second thing to do is to introduce yourself to 'country' and say 'hello' to the Old People (spirits) preferably in the local tongue if known and to refer to them by their Indigenous name. You also need to state your intention, in other words, the purpose of your visit and to ask permission to pass through. This is how I do it:

Nungamanladi (hello in Bardi) Wuradjuri (name of the local people). My name is Munya. I'm a Bardi woman from the Kimberley region of Western Australia. I want to visit this _____ cave/waterhole/ (whatever it is) to _____ (state what that is).

Is it all right for me to come through?

I then listen to my *lian* (spirit) and it lets me know if permission has been granted. This requires a form of *deep* listening (a practice I teach). I usually get a strong sense if permission is not given. If so, I indicate by gestures or words and simply move away.

You may ask: 'Why do I need to introduce myself?'

If you are passing through land for the first time, you are a *stranger* to it. The land doesn't know you. You therefore need to acknowledge the Old People (spirits) of the land on which you walk and introduce yourself. This is just being courteous and polite. This is a traditional cultural protocol that our people have always done. Even when we go swimming in a river or waterhole we introduce ourselves to country. One way of doing this is to rub the sweat from your underarm and place into the water before entering. That way the land can 'smell' you and know who you are. Following these protocols is not just about showing respect but providing a *safe passage* for you through country so that no harm will come to you.

Popular Walking Tracks

Aboriginal tracks and pathways are now signposted and made accessible to the public for all to enjoy. Many follow ancient songlines such as the Larapinta Trail near Mparntwe (Alice Springs) in the Northern Territory. This popular walk covers 223 kilometres from east to west, with the eastern end at Mparntwe and the western end at Mount Sonder along *Tjoritja* (the West MacDonnell Ranges).

A nine-day walking tour, the Lurujarri Heritage Trail, is run by the Goolarabooloo people in the Kimberley region of Western Australia. It stretches some 80km along the Rubibi (Broome) coastline that follows an important song cycle where Aboriginal guides share their heritage through stories and cultural activities. It is only conducted during *Barrgana* - the 'dry' season, so it is best to plan.

A much longer walk along the Bibbulmun Track of the

Noongar nation in the south-west of the state stretches an impressionable 1000km from Kalamunda in the Moroo (Perth) Hills, to Kinjarling (Albany) on the south coast. It is a walker-only trail that is divided into do-able segments. Although non-guided, it is clearly sign-posted and is well worth the effort. In addition to these walking trails there are several guided tours operated by Indigenous people throughout Australia where you can visit and learn about sacred sites and songlines. If you do go on these walks, please be respectful. If you follow the basic cultural protocols I've suggested you will be fine.

Sorry Rocks

Care should be taken when visiting country *not* to remove objects such as sand, seeds, shells, stones or twigs. Considered disrespectful, it not only distresses our people but causes grief for those who have taken these things. Visitors to Uluru are renowned for taking rocks and stones as souvenirs despite being asked not to by Parks Australia.[63] A surprising number of these are returned by mail from all over the world. Most are small pebbles, but some large rocks have also been mailed. The largest so far weighed a whopping 15 kilograms! The main reason they're given back is said to be out of a new-found respect for Indigenous culture but a small percentage have said they felt 'cursed' and had experienced bad luck since taking them. The local Anangu people call them *sorry rocks* because they are taken so far away from their homes that it makes people and the stones feel sad. It is like a relative being taken away or having died. Their name reveals our people's compassionate nature of feeling sorry for everything. For even though people have done the wrong thing by removing the stones, our mob still feel sorry that bad things have happened to the offenders as a result.

Collection of Sorry Rocks

Souvenir rocks are not only returned to Uluru but to other parts of the world. Parks Australia gives other examples where rocks are returned to their place of origin, such as lava rocks taken from Hawaii. As with Uluru, they are sent back for similar reasons, namely out of respect for the Goddess Pele and for the bad luck experienced by tourists after removing them. [64] The reason why our people consider it disrespectful to remove stones and other objects from the land or to damage it is because it disturbs the original markings of the Dreaming Beings who created the landscape. The only exception to this rule is the removal of crystals and ochre for Law Business or ceremonial use.

Former Australian of the Year, Galarrwuy Yunipingu explains this cultural prohibition in the following story when he was a 16-year-old boy:

"One day, I went fishing with Dad. As I was walking along behind him I was dragging my spear on the beach which was leaving a long line behind me. He told me to stop doing that. He continued telling me that if I made a mark, or dig, with no reason at all, I've been hurting the bones of the traditional people of that land. We must only dig and make marks on the ground when we perform or gather food." [65]

Leaving the land unmarked ensures it remains as it did on the First Day of creation. And while the land may change its appearance through the elements – bush fires, floods, rain and so on, these are seen to be the actions of nature *spirits* not caused by human intervention.

Dreamtime Reflections

1. Have you ever experienced feeling uncomfortable in the bush where you felt you should not be there? Did you listen to that feeling or did you fight it? Did anything happen when you resisted the feeling?
2. Do you know whose country you live or walk on? Try saying hello to the land and the Old People (spirits) as outlined on pp. 56 -57.
3. Try walking barefoot on the ground (not in Snake Country) and see if you are able to pick up any messages from the land.
4. Have you ever felt uneasy removing something from the land, and if so, what did you do to feel right again?
5. Love Magic – Is there anything you want to call into your life? Is it a baby? Do you want a special love relationship? Do you want financial abundance? Focus on your intent and paint this on a smooth river stone. Listen to some Aboriginal music as you are painting the stone or write your own song, giving praise to the Ancestors and thanking them for granting your wish. Place this stone somewhere special (not too far from where it came from) and bury it in the land. This act imitates planting a seed (guruwarri) that will grow to grant your wish.

Chapter 5
Rainbow Snake

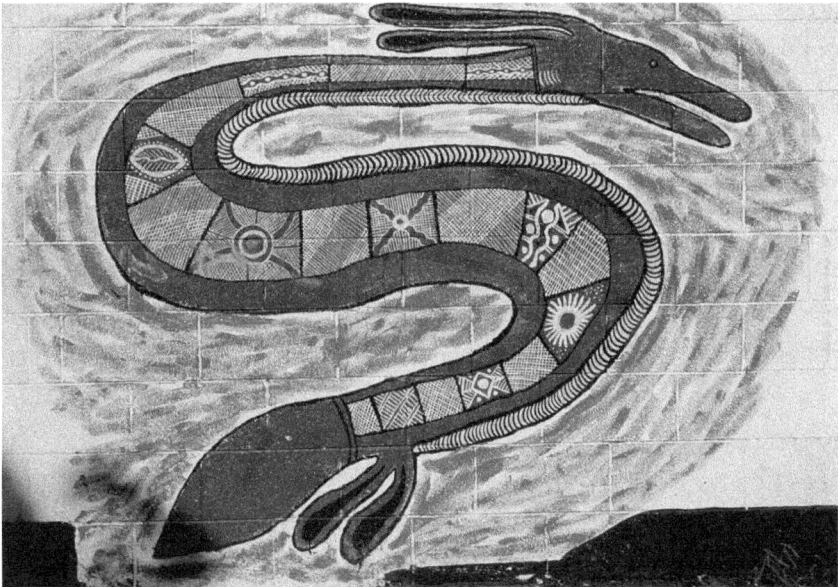

Rainbow Snake mural, Tiwi Islands

The Rainbow Snake is *the* most sacred of the ancestral creators in Aboriginal Australia. Highly venerated and deeply respected it plays a pivotal role in our spirituality. Despite being called by various names, it is commonly known by its colourful nickname in Aboriginal English. To the Gunwinku to the north east of Darwin it is *Ngalyod*. The Noongar of the south-west region of Western Australia call it *Wagyl* whereas the Warlpiri in the Northern Territory refer to it as *Warnayarra*. Even though stories of the

Rainbow Snake differ between the tribes, it shares many similar attributes and characteristics. Almost everywhere it is associated with creative and destructive forces and plays a key role in the healing arts. These stories are all about instructing young people in the mysteries of life that involve initiation and transformation.

Given Australian Aboriginal culture is said to be the world's longest continuing culture, the Rainbow Snake is arguably the oldest religious emblem in human history. While some of our mob may refer to it as 'he', in fact, it is bisexual. In other words, it is male and female. Only a Cleverman or Cleverwoman truly versed in traditional laws would be aware of this. The emphasis placed on either sex is just to emphasise the traits associated with that gender. It also reflects the gendered division of spiritual knowledge into 'men's business' and 'women's business' so prominent in Aboriginal culture. Neither one is more important than the other, they are complementary aspects of the same energy. In the past, male anthropologists ignored women's religious expertise, which was not fully appreciated or promoted.

Because of its fierce reputation, many Aboriginal people are afraid of the Rainbow Snake. Its name is so sacred that they will whisper it rather than say it out aloud. Or else they will simply refer to it as 'the Snake'. And even though it differs from ordinary snakes, people are reluctant to hurt snakes in general for fear they will draw its wrath. In some Indigenous cultures, there are strict rules prohibiting snakes being thrown in the campfire (other than for cooking and eating). At one cultural festival in the Kimberley in the 1980's, I witnessed such an unfortunate incident and the controversy it engendered. The poor offender was a young man from another nation who was unaware of this important protocol in that region.

Healing powers of the Snake

The Rainbow Snake plays a leading role in our healing

practices. Once again there are various names for healers. A common Aboriginal English term is 'bush doctor'. Likewise, traditional medicines are also referred to as 'bush medicine'. These men and women of 'high degree' are sought out by patients who will travel vast distances to engage their services. The snake is a popular motif in world cultures associated with healing. Almost everyone is familiar with the medical symbol of two snakes winding around a winged staff. Taken from Greek mythology, the caduceus represents the staff of the Olympian god Hermes. In fact, the Greek god of healing was Asclepius whose rod features a single snake. Most Aboriginal healers attribute their abilities to the Snake. But whereas people will go to a healer or bush doctor to be fixed, mabarn will go directly to the snake. In the book *Yorro Yorro*, Aboriginal Elder, David Mowarljarlai, tells the story of one such healer, a *banman* who was cured of leprosy by *Wunggud* who licked his sores clean and restored him to health. [66]

The Wawalag Sisters

The Rainbow Snake plays a central role in the initiation and transformation of the Wawalag Sisters of Arnhem Land who brought culture to their people. Like other Mother Goddesses in that area, the Wawalag Sisters named everything in their land and helped create the kinship system and sacred laws that men follow. The two women set out from the south, heading north to saltwater country. The older sister carried a small child with her, while the younger one was pregnant. Along the way, they hunt and kill numerous small animals and gather plant food to eat. On one of their stopovers, the younger sister gives birth to a son of the opposite moiety. They eventually stop at a sacred waterhole where they set up camp and cook their food on an open fire. Unbeknown to them, Julunggur the Snake is lying in wait in the deep. The older sister begins menstruating and some of her blood runs into the pool which stirs the Snake. He follows the trail of blood to discover the sisters sleeping with their children whereupon he swallows them. Although the Snake is male in this story, it has several female characteristics. It lies coiled in the waterhole, a symbolic uterus in waters associated with giving birth. Further, as the men re-enact the story in their initiation ceremony, they acknowledge and pay homage to the Wawalag Sisters who gave them the Law. This respectfully speaks to women's creativity and associates female power with the Snake. In many of these stories, She *is* the Snake. In my Dreamtime workshops, we explore this story in greater detail through creative exercises that leave you feeling connected and empowered.

Why is it called the Rainbow Snake?

In addition to healing, the Snake is credited with creative and destructive powers. Many Dreamtime stories tell how she created mountains, rivers and rock pools. People often ask, why is it called the 'Rainbow' Snake and how does it differ from an ordinary snake? Most commentators suggest it received its colourful name because of its association with rain and water. And as we know, wherever there are storm clouds, rainbows appear. This simple explanation provides yet another example of the difference between spiritual teachings for children and that for adults. In the children's version, the Rainbow Snake is associated with water, hence its name. But in the adult version, these stories touch upon deeper levels to unravel its secrets. As we saw earlier, knowledge in Aboriginal culture is either *outside* or *inside* as symbolised by the outer bark or inner heartwood of a tree. One of the reasons it receives its colourful nickname is not simply because of its association with water but because it carried a quartz crystal, which it used to create waterholes and burst its way through rocks and mountains. Therefore, the quartz crystal or *jagula* is the prized tool of our healers because of this association. Long before it became a New Age trend, Aboriginal people have been working with crystals for their healing properties for hundreds of thousands of years.

Like water, crystals are also linked to the rainbow. If you hold a quartz crystal to the light, you will see a rainbow coloured prism. And as we know, the rainbow spectrum is made up of seven rays of light that form one visible light. Given that the Rainbow Snake is a potent symbol of God (the snake itself is *not* God), I find it enormously intriguing that Jesus refers to himself as "The *Light* of the World" (John 8:12). Now some will say, "Yes but Munya, the light that Christ spoke of is 'spiritual' light - that which is illumination or enlightenment. Perhaps so, but allegory aside, it is *light* nonetheless. And the Rainbow Snake is the embodiment of its physical properties as well as its spiritual.

The Rainbow Snake is different from ordinary snakes because it is a metaphor of God whereas the others are not. Moreover, the Snake takes on mythical characteristics in paintings and stories such as its hermaphrodite nature or hybrid features. For example, the Caterpillar Dreaming that created the MacDonnell Ranges near Alice Springs in the Northern Territory is another aspect of the Rainbow Snake whose songline extends out into the Tiwi Islands north of Darwin. As it travels along the songline, it changes its physical features to emphasise the unique traits and qualities of both creatures whose spiritual meaning is closely guarded. The fact that it changes its shape to resemble other creatures speaks to the Oneness of creation - that we are all just diverse genetic expressions of the One consciousness or divine soul.

Organ Pipes National Park

My spiritual awakening first came as a young woman living in Perth in the 1980s. A staunch supporter of Indigenous rights,

I was active in the local Noongar community fighting for land and equal rights. While living in the Perth suburb of Nedlands along the Swan River, I had my first encounter with the Wagyl, as Noongar people call their sacred snake. Walking late at night by the foreshore I heard the strangest sound I had ever heard in my life. The voice followed me home where I later heard it emanating from under my bed. I spoke with a local Elder who confirmed it was Wagyl due to recent disturbances around the river. That was a 'vocal' encounter I had with the Rainbow Snake but it wasn't until I moved to Melbourne that I had a life-changing experience involving a vision. I first spotted the Organ Pipes National Park out of my plane window flying into Melbourne. I was drawn to a spot along a creek I spied. Upon landing I hurriedly looked up as close to the location that I estimated in the local street directory that led me to the park just outside Melbourne.

Organ Pipes National Park, Victoria

The Organ Pipes National Park is so named because its basalt columns resemble "the magnificent pipes of organs found in the world's grandest cathedrals." [67] And as a park brochure says, "This cathedral is a natural one, but no less awe-inspiring for that." [68] The towering columns rise 70 metres in a cliff-like structure with Jackson's Creek at its base. The columns are said to be made from molten lava one million years ago that cooled and cracked. The brochure states: "At ground level, a natural amphitheatre was created, providing a perfect spot from which to witness the glory of this amazing rock structure." [69] An appropriate accolade, this beautiful setting is where I encountered the glory and magnificence of the majestic Rainbow Snake.

When I first visited there some years ago, the park was not as established as it is now. Not much of the ground had been cleared and was bushier than it is today. After viewing the Tessellated Pavement and the Rosette Stone nearby, I sat down by Jackson's Creek directly opposite the Pipes. It was a warm sunny day and I found myself gently drifting off when I saw a vision of the sacred Snake. Like many Aboriginal people, I had been brought up with Dreamtime stories of the Rainbow Snake as a child but having experienced what I did, I now know they are not just 'stories'. The Snake I saw was a huge, luminescent, light green colour whose insides were transparent. Curiously, green is considered the prime colour of healing. As I looked inside the Snake I saw an orange-red glow like that of dying embers. If you've ever attended a lantern festival like the annual one held in Lismore in northern New South Wales, it resembled those magical papier-mâché figures lit within. I sat transfixed. How long, I don't remember, but I do know it touched something deep inside me and I was never the same. All I felt in that moment was an exquisite sense of joy, love and contentment. It was truly a case of being touched by the sacred. I have since returned many times to the park either accompanied by friends or alone but have never repeated the experience. Still, the memory of that moment of enlightenment has stayed with me through the years and I feel Her presence with me all the time. I am grateful for having been touched by what some might describe as 'God' and feel truly blessed.

Rainbow Snake Symbolism

Many have contemplated the symbolism of the Rainbow Snake to understand its true meaning. Some equate it to unseen cosmic energies that speak to our creation. Robert Lawlor, for example, likens the Rainbow Snake to the electromagnetic spectrum whose colours "is a profound metaphor for the unity that exists between the tangible and the invisible worlds." [70] In *Voices of the First Day*, he says all living things are bathed in this nourishing spirit whose serpentine energy "connects the earth with the celestial realms." [71]

Some see a direct correlation between the Snake and intertwining strands of DNA symbolised in the medical symbol of the Staff of Hermes or Caduceus. Karlene Strange takes the analysis to another level by bringing all these associations together - serpentine imagery together with the colours of the electromagnetic spectrum. In *The Spiritual Nature of Animals*, she says our DNA "emits photons at the spectrum of light" and that "this double-spiral, serpent-like molecule carries the genetic information or seed power present in every cell of every living thing, including bacteria, broccoli and bison." [72] Perhaps these ancient stories she says, "describe something we understand today with modern science." [73]

The Feathered Rainbow Serpent

Other writers have commented on the similarities between Quetzalcoatl (the feathered serpent of Aztec mythology), Kukulkan (Mayan feathered serpent), and the Rainbow Snake, but few realise just how alike they really are. Like Quetzalcoatl and Kukulkan, the Aboriginal Rainbow Snake is also feathered, it just isn't called that, openly at least. Once regarded as 'secret men's business' it has only become outed in recent years in public art exhibitions.

The feathered Rainbow Serpent is an ancient religious motif that combines two powerful individual creatures - the bird (usually an eagle) and the snake. To decipher its esoteric meaning is to consider snake-bird symbolism and imagery, their relationship to one another and their combined impact. Birds are creatures of the sky and as such are regarded as messengers from the spiritworld. Different species of birds extol special virtues. Just as the lion is said to be 'king' of the jungle, eagles are the lion kings of the bird world. Their keen eyesight, sharpened talons and hunting prowess make them a symbol of power and strength. They are a favoured mascot of the military for these reasons. Unlike birds, snakes are wedded to the earth and the underground. Many cultures perceive them as symbols of rebirth, transformation, immortality and healing. Their combination represents the union of these two worlds - earth and sky, which symbolises freedom to humans who are flightless and grounded. Curiously, some old astrology texts have identified three kinds of Scorpios, the highest of which is the Eagle Scorpio, which is a thinly disguised version of the snake (or reptile) bird combination. These individuals are said to be enlightened beings on a par with spiritual masters. The combined impact of these two creatures (bird and snake) is immortalised in stories around the world. Together they led to the foundation of Mexico City as depicted in their national flag that bears the image of a golden eagle perched on a cactus devouring a snake. This image is drawn from an Aztec legend of a leader who was visited in a dream by the god Huitzilopochtli. The god told him he would come across such a sight and it was there he was to build a great city which he did, calling it *Tenochtitlan*.

Here Be Dragons

In Asian and Celtic cultures, the feathered Rainbow Serpent is condensed into a single mythical beast, the dragon. While both cultures view this icon differently, it is simplistic to say that European cultures portray dragons as evil, fearsome and malevolent creatures whereas Asian cultures regard them as benevolent beings bestowing power, strength and good luck. In its takeover of the Celtic world, Christianity deliberately sought to destroy the old world pagan religion by portraying the dragon in a bad light. But in Celtic mythology dragons appear as guardians of wisdom and knowledge, having great vision and the power of prophecy. Symbols of supreme rule, the Celtic word for 'chief' is Pendragon as in Uther Pendragon, King Arthur's father, the head dragon. To walk with the dragon or the Rainbow Snake is to enter the world of magic.

Like the Dragon, the feathered Rainbow Snake is a commanding image with an equally powerful message to humanity. What it ultimately means is left to individual interpretation. To me, it represents unity between duality of earth and heaven, male and female as represented in the bisexual Snake. This union is reflected by the different colours of the rainbow that combine to form one light, one source. The journey we undertake to understand its true meaning is a journey of personal transformation and realisation. This ultimately leads to deep joy, deep ecstasy and deep connection. This elemental force comes straight from God the Source. It is all about becoming One with that power.

Dreamtime Reflections

1. How does a rainbow make you feel? What does the proverbial 'pot of gold' at the end of the rainbow signify to you?
2. What do birds symbolise to you?
3. What do snakes symbolise to you?
4. If you combine the two animals, what special qualities do they bring together? Does this increase your understanding of the Rainbow Snake?
5. What do dragons symbolise to you?

Chapter 6
Bush Doctors / Bush Medicine

Photo Credit: Regien Paassen - Shutterstock.com

Aboriginal Bush Doctor

There are as many Indigenous names for healers as there are nations, but a common Aboriginal English term is simply, 'Bush Doctor'. Likewise, traditional medicines are referred to as 'Bush Medicine'. We use the term *medicine* in a similar way that Native Americans do, as a medical system that encompasses a range of holistic treatments to treat illness or to promote health and wellbeing. We just insert the word 'bush' in front to emphasise that healing medicines and techniques not only come from the land but is informed by its Dreaming. *Banman* is a shared term used by the Worora, Wunambal and Ngarrinyin people in the Kimberley to refer to their healers [74] but I prefer the term *Mabarn* as used in the Pilbara and other parts of Western Australia. There is, however, some cultural sensitivity around the use of these terms. This is mainly because they are often used interchangeably with Aboriginal Law Men and Women, known as Clevermen and Cleverwoman. However, they are two quite distinct and separate roles. You do get situations where a Law Man or Law Woman may also be a healer but for the most part, they are regarded as separate fields of specialisation that require intensive, lifelong learning. Because of this degree of specialisation, they are held in such high regard that patients travel vast distances to engage their services. Even some *gudia* doctors and hospitals work alongside traditional healers to complement western treatment. [75] A newly opened Aboriginal Traditional Healing Centre (ANTAC) in Adelaide [76] provides a unique space where traditional healers (Ngangkari) offer individual healing sessions. Ngangkari share their culture and knowledge with anyone who is interested. It's well worth the visit to learn from these wise healers.

Even though health matters are classed as being 'men's' or 'women's business', both genders will go to see someone of the opposite sex. When it comes to bush medicine, a healer's reputation is more important than their gender. Most Aboriginal people prefer to be treated by a member of their own sex, which does not seem as important in the *gudia* system. Training for healers is long and intensive involving a range of processes and techniques. Even so, all healers credit the Rainbow Snake for their abilities. When it comes to healing themselves, mabarn go directly to the Snake.

The path to becoming a healer

A person's calling to become a healer differs among the various nations. Sometimes the ability to heal is handed down from one generation to another through their family Dreaming. People will say things like, "my mother or father before me was a healer and now it's my turn to carry on the tradition." Or it may be that a family member might inherit the healing Snake after a close relative dies who previously possessed that ability. It may be that someone undergoes a transformative or shamanic experience during an illness that brings valuable insight and further skills. For example, by communicating with spirits and journeying through *unseen* worlds they may be shown new medicines and treatments or learn new chants and songs. There is nothing quite like personal experience or insight that makes a great healer. Better still, having *Sickness Dreaming* provides a deeper understanding of sickness and healing that goes to the heart of its being. There are many places of Sickness Dreaming throughout Australia, most notably in areas with uranium deposits. Healers who carry this Dreaming have powerful medicine to live and walk in these places. They epitomise the biblical proverb, 'Physician heal thyself' (Luke 4:23).

Other than receiving a personal calling to become a healer, sometimes an Elder or Elders will recognise healing potential within someone, usually from a young age. When they do, they will encourage and guide that young person towards that profession. They will start subtly at first, making hints to him or her before passing on the 'tools of the trade' and actively seeking them out for healing. At first they may doubt their own ability and wonder why they are approached but are soon reassured by an Elder who will say something like: "You right. I *know* you can heal me. You got that *mabarn*."

The Ananagu people of the western desert refer to their healers as Ngangkari. One such healer, Maringka Burton describes how she became a Ngangkari:

"My father had been a Ngangkari his whole life, and his mapanpa (healing powers) had been given to him by his father. When he finally did give me the mapanpa, I became mara ala - meaning my hands became open, my forehead became open, and I could see everything differently. I was able to travel in the sky, just our spirits travelling, while our bodies remain sleeping on earth. My father taught me that. He taught me everything, carefully and slowly." [77]

The more encouragement a person receives, the more confident they become. They will then go on to serve as an apprentice with a senior healer to hone their skills to eventually become an adept. This may involve several initiation rituals in which a mabarn is made. These are different from rites of passage normally associated with the transition from adolescence to womanhood or manhood. Training to become a bush doctor can be an arduous process where the 'apprentice' must pass a series of harrowing challenges and trials. Much of this will involve psychic terror. An Aboriginal woman healer friend of mine, Violet Newman from Western Australia once said to me: "Munya, people have no idea of the work involved. It is so exhausting - the places I have to go and the things I have to do." She is referring to the unseen worlds she travels to and the things she encounters as a shamanic Cleverwoman.

Traditional Healing Tools and Practices

We saw in the last chapter, that the *jagula* or quartz crystal is the favoured tool of the Rainbow Snake and because mabarn get their abilities from the snake, it is their primary healing tool. Some mabarn have quartz crystals ritually inserted inside their bodies during their initiation. These enable them to have X-ray vision to diagnose illness, to see over vast distances (remote viewing), to see spirits, and travel to the Underworld to commune with them. *Gwan* or the Mother of Pearl, like the crystal is also used to heal because of its close association with the Snake. Its sheen is likened to lightning or lights flashing off the cheeks of the Rainbow Snake, who is closely linked to rain and water. In certain light you can see the colours of the rainbow reflecting off the shell. Bardi engrave and paint pearl shells with red ochre, which become sacred objects called *riji* or *jakuli*. These are traded far and wide and are prized for their healing and rain-making powers. Other stones besides crystals are used. These are called *ollumballu* or 'magic' stones. [78] Healers carry their magic stones and other healing tools in their dilly bags, which they use in treating patients.

Bush Doctor showing quartz crystal inserted in his tongue

Bush medicine includes the entire range of herbs and plants, including the use of powdered ochre which is used to treat an array of ailments. [79] Ochre is a natural clay earth pigment which is a mixture of ferric oxide and varying amounts of clay and sand. It comes in various shades of colour - black, brown, orange, purple, red and yellow. But of all the ochres, red is the most sacred because of its spiritual associations. It is so powerful, it is used sparingly to treat patients. It is most effective in treating eye conditions, insect bites, covering wounds, stopping bleeding and treating ulcers. It is also used to treat blood conditions, including cancer. Used in powder form it can be stirred in liquid and drunk. When animal fat is added, it can be used as a soothing balm or ointment that can be applied directly to sores and wounds. Ti tree and other oils are used as gentle treatment for babies, children and the elderly.

'Smoking' is also used to treat a patient. This does not involve cigarettes or tobacco. In Native American ceremonies, natural tobacco is powerful medicine and a sacred herb. *Smoking* is an Aboriginal English term for the purification of people and space where a ceremony is to be held. It involves placing the leaves of certain trees on fire before smothering it to create smoke that is 'brushed' on the ground or around a person's body. Sometimes bark is set alight rather than leaves in a small wooden container such as a coolamon that is waved around to create a similar effect. The choice of tree and bark used for smoking ceremonies varies among the nations. Native Americans also practise smoking ceremonies but usually with sage sticks (bundled sage leaves with a string handle) used to the same effect.

Bush Doctor treating his patient

Smoking ceremonies are usually performed by an Elder or healer. Smoke purifies by extracting negative energy from a person or place before releasing it to the spirits. Billowing smoke takes this negative energy up into the sky where it can disperse and not pollute the earth or the self. Sound therapy is also used in a similar way. The didjeridu is a powerful tool along with special chants and songs. As well as bringing medicine to the patient, playing the didjeridu is healing in and of itself. Many of the breathing techniques used to play the instrument are the same as yoga practices, such as Pranayama, which is the formal practice of controlling your breath. Mindful breathing creates a meditative state that facilitates healing at a deep level and creates altered states of consciousness that enable conversations with the spiritworld. Meditation and massage aid in healing, of which there are a variety of techniques. Paperbark is used to create poultices or to bandage wounds, while hair-string provides tourniquets to constrict or compress bleeding and to treat headaches. Group therapy is encouraged through ritual performances such as corroboree where everyone can participate and contribute to the healing process. Psychic surgery and the laying of hands is done by specialist healers.

Dance is another tool for connecting with the Spiritworld and healing through altered states of consciousness. Dance is especially good for discharging negative energies in dancer's bodies and in the spaces where they perform. This explains why Aboriginal men furiously stomp the ground when they dance, to discharge negative energies from their bodies by releasing it to Mother Earth for her to purify and cleanse. In return she gives personal power and strength to dancers that make them strong warriors to go out into the world. The continual act of purification through smoke and dance make corroboree grounds holy.

Unlike the men, women don't stomp when they dance. They do a shuffling movement along Mother Earth instead that imitates the Rainbow Snake. It puts her in touch with the *kundalini* energies of the Snake Goddess to do with sexual healing, the fertility of earth and self. Dancing creates a state of calmness and relaxation that allow things to flow. It alters our states of consciousness that allow us to feel and experience other worlds. It puts us in touch with the eternal Dreamtime. Culture makes us strong, say the Elders. It gives us all the tools and resources we need to cope with life. When culture is taken away from people or they are not allowed to practise it, it debilitates us and in extreme cases can break a person's spirit. We only need to look at the downtrodden, the disenfranchised, those seeking comfort in alcohol and drug abuse as their souls are crying out for emotional support and spiritual sustenance. Dreamtime is a path to well-being and wholeness that works on a multitude of levels.

Sickness Dreaming

What Aboriginal people call *Sickness Dreaming* refers to both a physical location or as someone's personal or family Dreaming such as Crocodile Dreaming or Yam Dreaming. Another way of distinguishing between the two kinds of Sickness Dreaming is to talk about *Sickness Country* that relates to place as opposed to healing powers that come from having this Dreaming. Visiting Sickness Country without cultural protection results in sickness. The illnesses vary in manifestation but are usually quite serious and can lead to death in some cases. Not surprisingly, many of these places are situated in areas of high deposits of uranium, especially at mining sites where it has been disturbed.

In the popular three-part documentary series, *Uranium - Twisting the Dragon's Tail*, Canadian physicist Derek Muller explores Aboriginal legends about uranium from the Kakadu region. Opening dramatically against the mystic backdrop of the Kakadu escarpment, we hear Muller's voice telling us, "Legends say there's a world beneath this one where a dragon lies sleeping.

They say be careful how you wake the dragon." [80] The 'dragon' in this case is none other than the sacred Rainbow Snake whose formidable powers of creation and destruction are revered and feared by our mob. Uranium has been mined in the Kakadu region since the 1950's. Muller closes this dramatic opening saying: "The Indigenous people here believe a powerful spirit sleeps beneath the ground and if disturbed will unleash catastrophe." [81]

Koongarra Traditional Owner, Jeffrey Lee talks to Muller about the powerful Sickness Dreaming which they call *Jungu*. He tells how when he walks around his lands he gets goose bumps and counsels: "You do not disturb. Do not touch anything...trees... anything that lives here in this country...we gotta stay away from it." [82] If the area is disturbed, the consequences may be quite severe says Lee. "You won't wake up the next day. That's the *jung*. It follows you around. I'm telling you - don't do anything around that country. And that's why me and my people (are) frightened." [83] A rock painting nearby is said to warn of the dangers of visiting sites or places they're not allowed to. Muller sees instead a dire warning of the toxic nature of uranium.

'Warning' Painting, Kakadu National Park

"This painting is really fascinating" says Muller. "It's an ancient health warning." Pointing to the swollen joints he says: "It shows the sickness you will contract if you disturb the stones in this area." [84]

Besides paintings that warn of the dangers of visiting sickness country, people can psychically sense whether they are safe or not. We are culturally primed to do this and have developed a keen sense of ESP known as *punka punkara*. This relates to the body as an entire communication system where each separate organ represents an individual family member. So, for example, if someone feels a throbbing in their upper arms it represents their parents. They know straight away that their mother or father is thinking of them or they will receive a message about either parent. When their leg or calf starts to throb that means your elder sister or brother is involved and they will hear from either sibling soon. Whistling in the ear signifies your older brother whereas crackling in the nose indicates a visitor. Heart palpitations symbolise their mother's brother or mother's brother's son. They know their uncle or male cousin is involved. Throbbing in the groin means your partner or spouse is thinking of you, which is not surprising given the fires of passion, and so on it goes.

The ability to acquire information on distant objects or people through the interpretation of physical disturbances of the body, such as throbbing, twitching, itching or whistling in the ears is a form of communication called telaesthesia. Although highly developed in our mob, it is not an unknown phenomenon even in the western world. Examples include itchy palms that relate to gaining (right palm) or losing money (left palm) or ringing in the ears (tinnitus) when people are talking about you.

In the Kimberley, we are taught at a young age to listen to our *lian* (spirit) or *gi*. This is the force within that protects us from harm. In the chapter on Sacred Sites, I shared what happened to me when I didn't listen to my *lian*. Someone that did listen to his spirit was famous Australian painter Arthur Boyd. I recall watching a television interview he did in the 1980s. He told a story of how he was painting out in the bush near Mparntwe (Alice Springs) in the Northern Territory. It was twilight, the sun had just set and Boyd was finishing his painting when he felt this strong sense that he should not be there. He didn't understand why there was this pressing feeling that he should leave immediately but he trusted his instinct. Hurriedly bundling up his easel, paints and brushes he bolted out of there. He later described it as a warning. Other people have told me similar stories. I was always taught to respect the bush, to listen and be mindful. While it is a source of great strength and can give you power, it also teaches humility for us to know our place in the great scheme of things. The feelings of danger you get may be country looking after and protecting you.

Sacred objects and being 'sung'

Sometimes people can get sick from viewing or touching restricted objects such as those used for Law Business or not following proper protocols. Certain cultural objects are imbued with supernatural powers because of being sung or used in ceremonies. Many are inscribed or painted with sacred designs such as Tjurunga (pronounced churunga), also referred to as 'bullroarers'. Tjurunga are incised boards or stones used in ceremonies. [85] They symbolise Dreamtime Beings that bring fertility and strength to individuals and the entire community. When not in use, they are hidden in caves or some other secret location where they are protected. Tjurunga is an Aranda word for 'sacred', which reveals the esteem in which they are held. Strict rules prohibit these objects being shown to outsiders or the uninitiated who may suffer harm consequently. As with all sacred objects and powers, they can be used for good or evil.

Like other zealously guarded knowledge, a secrecy code operates regarding Dreamtime traditions. If an Aboriginal person starts to talk about secret law matters in public, the Elders will give them the 'hard eye' or some other sign to let them know they are treading on dangerous grounds. They know straight away when they are crossing the line or if not, they will find out soon enough. Serious transgressions or wrongdoing is dealt with by *kadaitcha* or 'Featherfoot' man, so named for the special shoes they wear made of emu feathers that leave no footprints. The chants and songs they sing reputedly enables them to manipulate time and space so that they can travel over enormous distances in a short period.

Besides unlawful touching of sacred objects, people can also get sick from being 'sung'. This involves the use of sorcery such as 'pointing the bone' at someone to make them sick. Whatever your thoughts on the subject, the simple fact remains - many of our mob believe this can affect their mental and physical wellbeing. Personally, I believe that we are *powerful* beings and that we can only be hurt when we give our power away. The misuse of power for evil purposes is wrong no matter what creed or political persuasion, but we need not be afraid.

Sickness Dreaming Immunity

One example of personal empowerment is the notion of immunity to Sickness Dreaming. Near Mount Bomford on the Mitchell Plateau in the Kimberley is a site called *Mandjilwa*. Its Aboriginal English name is 'Guts Ache' because of the severe diarrhoea with blood people experience after visiting there. Mandjilwa is so strong that people can die just by being near it. [86] Sickness Dreaming is powerful to have because of the immunity and protection it gives to the individual and their loved ones. It also adds a higher level of degree and expertise to that healer because they understand sickness on a deeper, intimate and profound level. As David Mowarljarlai explains: "We have no Dreamings for healing, only plenty of Sickness Dreamings. When we are the owner of such a place and we go there, we don't get sick because we *are* that sickness, that painting, and immune to ourselves. We just *represent* that sickness." [87]

The idea of 'representing' sickness is radically empowering. It puts us in the driver's seat when it comes to our health and making our lives better. It is not reliant on an outside agent be it the medical profession or chemicals. It reminds us of the body's healing powers, of our personal ability to effect real change and transform our lives.

As with many Indigenous cultures, the Aboriginal approach to health and well-being is holistic. Being healthy means being of sound mind, body and spirit. Cultural explanations for poor health and sickness differ quite considerably from Western medicine, which has enormous implications for treatment. Sickness is viewed as the result of an individual not having followed proper protocols or as the direct result of another person's interference through sorcery. Care should be taken to not dismiss these perceptions and beliefs as 'superstition' or nonsense. They are *cultural* explanations that may differ dramatically from western perceptions but are just as valid.

As humans, all we have are our stories. It's how we make sense of them that matters. We can think of disease as pathological requiring medical intervention or we can approach it holistically. While it's important to acknowledge the medical benefits that western medicine can bring, it's equally important to deal with the broader issues at play. Diseases, like cancer for example, are not seen as a 'battle' to be fought or 'fight' to be won in Indigenous cultures but as a friend that brings an important spiritual message and gift to you. Doesn't it make sense to befriend rather than curse it? A more empowering approach to cancer or any other disease, whether life-threatening or not is to talk to it as you would a friend. Welcome that disease into your life. Invite it to sit down with you and ask what lessons it has brought you. It is not a stranger. It lives inside you and is *part* of you. Deep down you understand its Dreaming and with understanding comes *acceptance*. Healer, heal thyself.

Dreamtime Reflections

1. Can you identify a health issue that may be classified as women's business?
2. Can you identify a health issue that may be classified as men's business?
3. What special qualities does a healer have?
4. How does dancing or singing make you feel better?
5. How can you befriend 'disease' or illness in your body? What might it be telling you?

Chapter 7
Kindredness

Young Aboriginal Boys with Skin Body Paintings

In the Aboriginal worldview, all things are interrelated and interconnected with one another. In other words, everyone and everything is considered *family* - animals, trees, rocks and stars. The traditional concept to express this all-embracing, all-encompassing view of kinship is the Aboriginal English expression 'Skin'. All cultures have their own kinship patterns, rules and structures that reveal deep attitudes about kindredness and belonging in that society. Our notions of family are more aligned with other Indigenous people such as Torres Strait Islander, Maori and Native Americans.

How does 'skin' relate to kinship?

Just like Scottish families whose tartan designs are specific to family clans, Aboriginal people paint their clan or family designs on their bodies (instead of wearing marked clothing such as tartans) when they take part in corroboree, hence the origin of the term 'skin' to signify family ties. Once again, word play reveals a curious coincidence as 'kin' makes up part of the word 'skin'. Although the term 'skin' is mostly used in northern Australia, the skin concept is generally understood throughout the country by other names. For instance, the Aboriginal English term 'meat' was once used in New South Wales by Indigenous people to refer to their family groups in similar fashion. [88] It's important to not confuse Skin with skin colour. It has nothing to do with colour. It has everything to do with the relationships of individuals and groups within a tribe or nation who share a common language and social identity.

There is another level to Skin that relates to how we perceive and interact with our material world. We saw earlier that knowledge in Aboriginal culture is regarded as being an inside or outside phenomenon as depicted by the inner heartwood of a tree or its outside covering - the bark or skin of a tree. In *The Book of Symbols*, Karen Martin writes, "Skin is a tactile, responsive boundary between self and other, and the inside and outside of the individual." [89] What this means, is that we carry these two distinct layers of awareness and consciousness within our own bodies. As we journey through life and during our moments of epiphany and spiritual insight we move between the seven layers of skin to reach that place of ultimate *knowing*. In other words, we carry the Dreaming within. The tree is just an outer symbol for what we already know to be true. The other fascinating revelation is that our skin develops from "the same fetal tissue as the brain." [90] Could this mean we walk around wearing our intelligence on the outside? Perhaps this explains our psychic sensibilities that can read people, situations and our environment in an incredibly, intelligent and sentient way.

Moieties

At the heart of Aboriginal kinship are the marriage laws that strictly determine who can marry whom. From this basic relationship, all others flow. To begin with, all Indigenous nations divide their groups into two halves called *moieties* by anthropologists (French for 'half'). Their names differ according to the language groups but basically operate the same way. So, for instance, people will refer to themselves as either the 'Red Paint' mob versus 'White Paint' as in the Kimberley, or as 'East Wind' and 'West Wind' mob of Arnhem Land or as 'Eagle' mob versus 'Crow' in the southern regions. This means that 'community business'[91] or matters are divided between the moieties. So, only one moiety is responsible for 'sorry business' such as death, dying and funerals while the other moiety is responsible for birthing matters such as conception, love magic etc. All other community business will fall under one or other of the two moieties. This is important to note because the moieties and skin groups determine who can speak for country, songs, stories and so on. This is because as we have already seen, knowledge is not a freely available commodity in Aboriginal society. Access is governed by age, gender and skin or clan membership.

Skin Groups

After this basic moiety division, the group is further divided into smaller groups, each having their own skin names that sit under one of the two moieties. The actual number of skin groups vary between the tribes and increase exponentially from 2, 4, 8, 16, 32 and 64. So any individual nation will have one of these numbered skin systems. According to this system, people can only marry a person of the opposite moiety and even then, only one other skin group who they refer to as being 'straight for' them (because they are directly opposite). In the Kukatja Skin system diagram, the spousal line is represented by the dotted line. This is the preferred or ideal situation. However, being human means there are likely to be star-crossed lovers sometimes. Therefore, some skin systems will allow a person to marry one other skin group (such as cross-cousin) but only as a last resort to avoid *wrong way* marriage or *poison* relationships. The reason for strict adherence to the skin system was a means of keeping the blood lines pure to avoid genetic complications that result from marrying close kin.

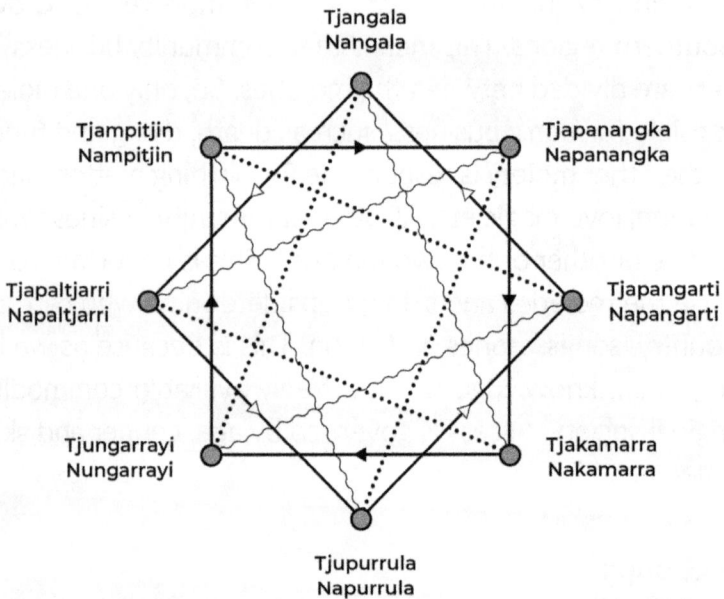

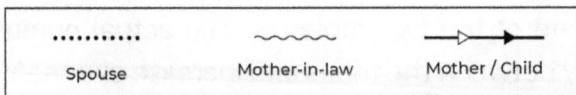

Kukutja Skin

Everyone is Family

The skin systems follow a set pattern laid down in the Dreamtime that reveal how everyone in that nation is related to one another and the exact nature of that relationship e.g. mother, father, husband, wife, daughter, son, aunty, uncle, cousins, grandparents and so on. They not only vary according to number but to gender. In the *Kukutja* system of the Kimberley [92] for example, although there are 8 skin groups, in total there are 16 because there are two subsets within each skin group, i.e. one for each sex. The male skin group names begin with Tj as in Tjampitjin, Tjangala and Tjakamarra and the female skin groups begin with Na as in Nampitjin, Nangala and Nakamarra. So, your skin name reveals whether you are a man or a woman. Not all Aboriginal skin systems make this distinction on gender obvious. Skin systems are either matrilineal, meaning that children inherit their skin names through the mother (as in the Kukutja system) or they are patrilineal, in which case the children get their skin name from the father. And just to add to the confusion, some skin systems are ambilineal, in which case they obtain skin names through the mother *and* father!

Many Mothers and Fathers

Essentially, children are born into a different skin group than that of their parents. Grandparents and grandchildren however share the same skin name, which is why grandparents call their grandchildren *grannies* in Aboriginal English. And because skin divides the entire tribe into set groups having designated kinship roles, there will be whole groups of people in one category or another. This explains why an Indigenous person can have many mothers, fathers, brothers, sisters, uncles, aunties, cousins and grandparents. Not all are biological relationships, they include social relatives; those that are not blood-related. But social relatives are no less important than biological ones. So, if a social grandmother passes, it is just as important to go to her funeral as it is for a biological grandmother.

From the Kukutja Skin diagram we can see how there are many mothers and fathers. The straight arrow lines indicate the mother/child relationship. What this means is that your mother or child will belong to a specific skin group different from each other. It also means that while your mother may be Nakamarra, all the other women in that skin group are also your mothers and vice versa, all the children in a certain skin group will be your children. They will call you 'mum' and in turn you will call them 'son' or 'daughter'. According to this diagram, they are Tjungarrayi and Nungarrayi if the mother is Nakmarra. But if you are a Napangarti woman in the diagram, your son and daughter will not be Tjupurrula and Napurrula because the arrow points in the *other* direction. In other words, your children will be Tjangala and Nangala (son and daughter). The Kukutja Skin system is matrilineal, which means that children inherit their skin names from the mother, not from the father. Just like the Jewish tradition, which dictates that you can only call yourself Jewish if your mother is Jewish (not your father), this Skin system operates in the same way.

One's skin group also determines one's family or group Dreaming. For example, in the *Kukutja* skin system of the Kimberley, the male *Tjakamarra* group's Dreaming is the Orion constellation whereas the female *Nakamarra* skin group's Dreaming is the Seven Sisters or the Pleiades star cluster. [93] What this means is that members of those skin groups are primarily responsible for all the songs, stories and ceremonies to do with that Dreaming. In other words, they are the only ones that can speak for or about matters to do with those stars.

Marrying Wrong Way

The consequences for marrying wrong way are not as severe as they once were. In the past, star-crossed lovers were banished by their tribe and left to fend for themselves. Nowadays, even though the punishment is less severe, not following the rules is still frowned upon. Having said that, the recent six-part investigative podcast series *Wrong Skin* by the Melbourne Age has raised the issue of what is the appropriate punishment for two young lovers who broke the Law. Investigative journalist, Richard Baker has re-examined a murder cold case from Looma in the Kimberley that involved a *wrong way* relationship. While the podcast has led to reopening the cold case, it is a perfect example of the abuse and misuse of power for evil purposes. I wrote an opinion piece on the issue that was published in the Melbourne Age in 2018 denouncing and questioning cultural excuses for this crime. To date, the perpetrator or perpetrators have not been identified or charged and the murder case remains a mystery. What the case illustrates is how religion can be used to justify or rationalise almost *any* wrongdoing and that is wrong. And it's not just serious crimes as rape or murder but the harms we commit against each other daily.

Taboo Relationships

Some relationships in Aboriginal society are considered taboo, which means that there are certain restrictions prohibiting people from engaging and interacting with one another. For example, wrong-way marriages are often described as *poison*. The most famous of these is the mother-in-law relationship. In Aboriginal culture, a man or woman is not allowed to talk to their mother-in-law and vice versa – she is not allowed to speak to them! Communication through a third party is acceptable. The prohibition sometimes extends to other in-law relationships like father-in-law, sister and brother-in-law and so on. But the strongest prohibition concerns the mother-in-law. In the Kukutja Skin diagram, you can trace the mother-in-law relationship by following the squiggly lines.

When other people first discover this cultural protocol, they are naturally curious why this came about. A common explanation surrounds promised marriages. Traditionally, a young girl would be promised to a much older man. What this means is that the so-called 'son-in-law' would very likely be of the same age as the wife's mother and therefore make them peers. Because the Skin system is devised to prevent inter-breeding, the mother-in-law prohibition guards against the possibility or likelihood of these two peers engaging in an intimate, sexual relationship with one another.

When people play the Skin Game with me, we go through the complexity of Aboriginal family relationships where people gain deeper appreciation and understanding of Aboriginal culture.

The Living Mandala

In addition to a teaching aid, the Aboriginal mandala can also be used as a spiritual tool that operates at the physical level. For Aboriginal people, ours is a *living* mandala, not just a pretty drawing. The spiritual insights one gains by literally walking the perimeters of the Skin Mandala (i.e. by living and breathing it through *real* live relationships) are more powerful than gained through meditating and reflecting on its physical structure alone. Having said that and not withstanding its spiritual aspects, Skin serves as a scientific model for Indigenous astronomy, genetics and mathematics. As a child growing up in the Kimberley, old people would point to the Blue Mountain parrot or Rainbow lorikeet and say to me, "Munya, if you marry wrong way, your children will end up like that." No, not as a bird (go with the abstract concept) but with genetic complications as the multi-coloured bird. This instruction shows we had good understanding of genetics and the medical complications that can arise from marrying too close. It's something the Royal Families of Europe could well have learned from our mob but they have another agenda altogether! Skin demonstrates the complexity and ingenuity of Aboriginal cultures.

We saw earlier that the skin group you belong to determines your family Dreaming. The example given was that of Tjakamarra and Nakamarra men and women having Star Dreaming relating to the Orion constellation and Pleiades star cluster respectively. This is because just like Dreaming, everyone and everything fits into the Skin system and are in relationship to each other, including the stars. So, Skin also teaches us astronomy. I once attended a CSIRO (Commonwealth Scientific and Industrial Research Organisation) conference in northern Queensland on Indigenous knowledge. Murri artist Karen Williams gave a slide presentation of her paintings of the stars based on Dreamtime stories she was told as a child. One slide showed her painting of the Southern Cross constellation (*Crux Australis*), which is her family Dreaming. The astounding thing was, it showed the view not from Earth looking toward the Southern Cross but the opposite direction! The mind boggles at just how far Aboriginal Dreamings and Songlines extend and what amazing information they contain.

Gudia are only just beginning to find out about our sciences. One of the reasons why Indigenous cultures aren't recognised as clever is because unlike western cultures our technology is *hidden* whereas western technology is external, visible and tangible. We can walk around the Colosseum or the Taj Mahal and marvel at the sheer beauty and mathematics of its architecture, but Skin is not as obvious although no less technical. In my Skin workshops, I can walk you through its cleverness and complexity, and you will be astounded. When teaching and instructing our young in Dreamtime Laws and our sciences, we turn to our environment and tools that lie within such as the Skin Birds or Blue Mountain parrots. Every living thing, animate or non-inanimate is a lesson to be taught with much wisdom to impart.

Skin Bird (Blue Mountain Parrot)

Everything is of significance where nothing is left to chance or coincidence. If a crow comes and sits on your fence, it brings news of someone's death and looming Sorry Business. It is not because they are vultures and can smell decomposing flesh as a friend of mine suggested. To focus purely on the material world is to ignore the *Otherworld* of the Dreamtime that science cannot explain. In the case of bringing sad news of a loved one's impending demise, Brother Crow might be hundreds of kilometres away from a decomposing body. Surely its smelling ability is not that keen! The same goes with the Mopoke owl on the east coast, the bearer of tragic news.

Finally, the Skin system is a mathematical model whereby all kindred relations can be written in formulae using algebra, arithmetic, geometry and trigonometry to name a few. When teachers or other people tell me that Indigenous kids aren't good at mathematics or science, I say to them, "It depends on what cultural models you're using to teach." If they only worked with Indigenous paradigms such as Skin, they would see great improvement.

The Relevance of Skin Today

All cultures evolve and change over time. The greater the influence, the faster a culture changes. Aboriginal society is no exception. Our influences include the Macassan sailors who travelled to Australia from Indonesia, and the English, Dutch, German, Irish and other European nations that have impacted Australia's colonial history. While colonisation has had a devastating impact on our mob, the *values* that make us distinctly 'Aboriginal' as opposed to Asian or European remains.

Even though some kinship systems have been lost or disrupted because of colonisation, you still find our mob relating to each other along traditional Skin lines. The only difference now is that English kinship terms are used such as mother, father, brother, sister, uncle, aunt and so on. It is customary to refer to older Aboriginal people as *Aunty* or

Uncle as a mark of respect. It doesn't mean they are an Elder. Not all aunties and uncles are Elders but all Elders are aunties and uncles. Elder status is not dependant on age but on the spiritual knowledge that one possesses. I'm often asked if it is okay to refer to an older Aboriginal person as 'Aunty' or 'Uncle'. Generally, it is not an issue and most of our mob are pleased at being shown respect in this way, but I would check beforehand to see whether an individual is okay with that or not. In all my travels around Australia, I have only ever come across one older Indigenous woman who objected to being called 'Aunty'. I recall the first time I was addressed as 'Aunty' was when I was teaching at Curtin University in Perth and a young Aboriginal man passed me by and said, "Hello Aunt". It's quite funny because I turned to look behind me to see who he was talking to! When I realised it was me, I had a little chuckle because I had somehow forgotten that I have aged and am now recognised as an Aunty in community. This concept of everyone being related to one another and the values of *belonging* is still alive despite colonial disruption or influence. It tells of the power of Indigenous resilience, which is a beautiful thing.

What can we learn from Aboriginal Skin and Dreamtime?

Australian Aboriginal culture and spirituality has much to offer humanity. Dreamtime is an ethics code that teaches respect for all things and being mindful of the consequences of our actions and behaviour on those we share our planet with - the creatures, rocks, rivers, trees and mountains. This world is not just ours to possess and do with as we please. We share it with other beings and have an obligation to look after it and leave it a better place for you and me.

An important message that Skin imparts is that we are all

related to each other and are *family*. And as family it would behove us to treat each other kindlier. This broader sense of kinship extends to animals, plants and so-called inanimate objects with whom we share our planet. The idea that we are more intimately connected or related to our fellow creatures (and the Universe in which we live) is a central precept of many Indigenous cultures. It is beautifully expressed in the totemic nature of Aboriginal Dreamtime and Native American spirituality. The Lakota end all their prayers with the phrase *Mitakuye Oyasin*, 'all my relations' to acknowledge our kinship and connection with all living beings with whom we share a common ancestry and destiny. Thus, when an Indigenous person proudly talks about their Kangaroo or Possum or some other animal or plant Dreaming, they are trying to convey a profound connection with that animal or plant. That kangaroo, possum or Ti tree may be an Elder, Teacher, Mother, Father, Brother, Sister, Son or Daughter, and as with any family or tribe, there is a deep, abiding sense of *community* with all the nuances that relationship entails. This inexplicable feeling of *kindredness* that Indigenous people feel towards their fellow creatures and their environment is a beautiful thing to be cherished.

It is our gift to the world.

Dreamtime Reflections

1. What is your understanding of Skin?
2. If your Skin name is Nakamarra, are you male or female?
3. Which Australian bird symbolises the kinship system?
4. If you were related to everyone in your community, how different would your life be? How does it feel to

consider an enemy or opponent as family? Does that change how you behave towards them?

5. Have you ever felt kinship with an animal, plant or star? What did it feel like? If you could characterise the relationship along family lines, what would it be, e.g. brother, sister, teacher, friend?

Suggested Readings

Munya Andrews, *The Seven Sisters of the Pleiades*, Spinifex Press, 2004.

Munya Andrews, "Jillinya: Mother Goddess of the Kimberley" in Patricia Monaghan (ed), *Goddesses in World Culture*, Volumes 1-3, Praeger, 2011.

Joseph Campbell, *The Power of Myth*, Doubleday, 1998.

John Cawte, *Healers of Arnhem Land*, University of New South Wales Press, 1996.

Bruce Chatwin, *The Songlines*, Vintage Publishing, 2010.

Emile Durkheim, *The Elementary Forms of Religious Life*, edited and translated by Karen E. Fields, The Free Press, 1995.

Clarissa Pinkola Estes, *Women Who Run With The Wolves*, Ballantine Books, 1992.

Gracie Greene, Joe Trammachi and Lucille Gill, *Tjarany Roughtail: The Dreaming of the Roughtail and Other stories*, Magabala Books, 2000.

Carl Jung, *Memories, Dreams and Reflections*, Fontana Press, 1961.

Robert Lawlor, *Voices of the First Day: Awakening in the Aboriginal Dreamtime*, Inner Traditions, 1991.

Tim Lowe, *Bush Medicine: A Pharmacopeia of Natural Remedies*, Angus & Robertson, 1990.

Kathleen Martin (ed), *The Book of Symbols*, Taschen, 2010.

David Mowarljarlai & Jutta Malnic, *Yorro Yorro*, Magabala Books, 1993.

Helen Milroy et al, *Traditional Healers of the Central Desert: Ngangkari*, NPY Women's Council Aboriginal Corporation, 2013

Deborah Bird Rose, *Dingo Makes Us Human*, Cambridge University Press, 2000.

Deborah Rose, Diana James and Christine Watson, *Indigenous Kinship with the Natural World in New South Wales*, NSW National Parks and Wildlife Service, 2003.

Carlo Rovelli, *The Order of Time*, Riverhead Books, 2018.

Peter Sutton, *Dreamings: The Art of Aboriginal Australia*, Penguin Books, 1988.

W.E.H. Stanner, *The Dreaming & Other Essays*, Black Ink Agenda, 1979.

Euan J. Squires, *The Mystery of the Quantum World*, Taylor & Francis Group, 1994.

Karlene Strange, *The Spiritual Nature of Animals*, New World Library, 2017.

References

Chapter 1. What is the Dreamtime?

1   Joseph Campbell, *The Power of Myth*, pp. 24-25. Kindle Edition.

2   Peter Sutton, *Dreamings: The Art of Aboriginal Australia*, p.15.

3   David Mowarljarlai & Jutta Malnic, *Yorro Yorro*, p.38.

4   Carl Jung, Memories, *Dreams and Reflections*.

5   Joseph Campbell, *The Power of Myth by Joseph Campbell*, p. 49. Kindle Edition.

6   David Mowarljarlai & Jutta Malnic, Yorro Yorro, p. 165.

7   From an interview with Trevor Wie by James Barty on *The Cosmic Switchboard Show*, YouTube channel, 15 December 2017.

8   Ibid.

9   Ibid.

10   S.W.O.T. = Strengths, Weaknesses, Opportunities and Threats.

11   Joseph Campbell, *The Power of Myth*, p. 18. Kindle Edition.

12   Ibid, p. 19.

13   See Carlos Rovelli, *The Order of Time*. This quote taken from the article, 'solving the Mystery of Time Flow – An Excerpt from The Order of Time," in *Science Friday* (Online).

14   Andrew Anthony, "What if we're living in a computer simulation?", *The Guardian* (Online), 22 April 2017.

15   Kevin Loria, "Neil deGrasse Tyson thinks there's a very 'high chance' the universe is just a simulation", *Business Insider* (Online), 6 March 2016.

16   Karen Martin, *Book of Symbols*, p. 706.

17   Michael Garett, *Walking On The Wind*, p. 615. Kindle Edition.

18   Ibid.

Chapter 2. Laying Down The Law

19   W.E.H Stanner, *The Dreaming and Other Essays.*

20   Author unknown, "The Carbon System of Law", Online article, no publication details.

21   Ibid.

22   Ibid.

23   Ibid.

24   David Mowarljarlai & Jutta Malnic, *Yorro Yorro*, p. 198.

25   See article "The Carbon System of Law," (Online) Unknown Author.

26   *Yorro Yorro*, p.150.

27   Ibid.

28   See Suzanne Simard's TED talk, "How Trees Talk to Each Other", 22 July 2016.

29   Karen Martin (ed), *The Book of Symbols*, p. 130.

30   "Pukumani poles from the Tiwi Islands," Australian Museum (Online), p. 2.

31   Ibid.

32   Munya Andrews, "Jillinya: Mother Goddess of the Kimberley" in *Goddesses of the World*, Vol. 3, edited by Patricia Monaghan, pp. 1-12.

33   *Terminalia carpentariae.*

34   Robert Lawlor, *Voices of the First Day*, p. 1.

35   Ibid.

36   Karen Martin (ed) *The Book of Symbols*, p. 396. For the original see Carl Jung, The Collected Works, Volumes 1-20.

37   From an interview with Trevor Wie by James Barty on *The Cosmic Switchboard Show*, YouTube channel, 15 December 2017.

38   Joseph Campbell, *The Power of Myth by Joseph Campbell*, p. 68. Kindle Edition.

39   Ibid, pp. 68-69.

40   Ibid, p. 69.

41   See Clarissa Pinkola Estes, *Women Who Run With The Wolves*, *Kindle Edition*

42   Ibid, pp. 386-387.

Chapter 3. Songlines

43   See Bruce Chatwin, *The Songlines*.

44   Jawi is another Indigenous nation with close cultural and family ties with Bardi people and who share country in common with each other, namely some of the islands and water channels.

45   Personal conversation.

46   David Mowarljarlai and Jutta Malnic, *Yorro Yorro*, p. 79.

47   *Dadirri* video, Miriam Rose Foundation, 2015.

48   Michael Garrett, *Walking On The Wind*, in the chapter on "The Rule of Acceptance".

49   Melissa Daimler, "Listening is an Overlooked Leadership Tool," *Harvard Business Review*, May 10, 2016.

50   Ibid.

51   Ibid.

52   Ibid.

53   Carl Jung, *Memories, Dreams and Reflections*, p. 20.

54   Ibid.

Chapter 4. Sacred Sites

55   See the Hindmarsh Island Bridge Controversy article in Wikipedia for a summary of the case that involved an Australian Royal Commission and a series of lawsuits.

56   Gi is pronounced as 'ghee'. It is like the Chinese word 'chi' to signify energies as in the meditation practice of Tai chi.

57   David Mowarljarlai & Jutta Malnic, *Yorro Yorro*, p. 67.

58   See "Nicole Kidman says fertility waters got her Pregnant", *Marie Claire*, September 14,2008.

59   Robert Lawlor, *Voices of the First Day*, p. 1.

60   Ibid.

61   Euan J. Squires, *The Mystery of the Quantum World*.

62   David Mowarljarlai & Jutta Malnic, *Yorro Yorro*, pp. 67-68.

63   See Uluru-Kata Tjuta National Park Factsheet, "Sorry Rocks" Parks Australia 2015.

64   Ibid.

65   Peter Sutton, Dreamings: *The Art of Aboriginal Dreamtime*, pp 13-14.

Chapter 5. Rainbow Snake

66   David Mowarljarlai & Jutta Malnic, *Yorro Yorro*, p. 178.

67   See Factsheet "Organ Pipes National Park: The outdoor cathedral," Parks Victoria 2018.

68   Ibid.

69   Ibid.

70   Robert Lawlor, *Voices of the First Day*, p. 115.

71   Ibid.

72   Karlene Strange, *The Spiritual Nature of Animals*, p. 36.

73   Ibid.

Chapter 6. Bush Doctors / Bush Medicine

74   David Mowarljarlai and Jutta Malnic, Yorro Yorro, p. 4.

75   See online article "Ngangkari healers: 60,000 years of traditional Aboriginal methods make headway in medical clinics," by Sowaiba Hanifie, 28 March 2018.

76   ANTAC stands for Anangu Ngangkari Tjutaku Aboriginal Corporation.

77   See newspaper article, "Super powers of central Australia's traditional healers", *The Australian*, 18 May, 2013.

78   David Mowarljarlai & Jutta Malnic, *Yorro Yorro*, p. 221.

79   See Tim Lowe, *Bush Medicine: A Pharmacopeia of Natural Remedies* for further information.

80   See the television documentary series *Uranium – Twisting the Dragon's Tail*, Genepool Productions, 2015.

81   Ibid.

82   Ibid.

83   Ibid.

84   Ibid.

85   Peter Sutton, *Dreamings: The Art of Aboriginal Australia*, p. 92.

86   David Mowarljarlai & Jutta Malnic, *Yorro Yorro*, p. 43.

87   Ibid, p. 81.

Chapter 7. Kindredness

88   Deborah Rose et al, *Indigenous Kinship with the Natural World in New South Wales*, p. 25.

89   Karen Martin (ed), *Book of Symbols*, p. 338.

90   Ibid.

91   'Business' is an Aboriginal English word that doesn't refer

to economic transactions as it does in the western world but rather to everyday community matters and issues.

92   Gracie Greene, Joe Trammachi and Lucille Gill, *Tjarany Roughtail: The Dreaming of the Roughtail and Other stories* that explains the Kukutja Skin system.

93   Ibid.

About the Author

Munya Andrews is an Indigenous woman from the Kimberley region of Western Australia. Born to an Aboriginal mother and Scottish father, she is proud of her Aboriginal and Celtic heritage. Her Bardi 'saltwater' people come from the Dampier Peninsula and the offshore islands north of Broome.

Her early childhood was one of severe disadvantage, including isolation, poverty, sexual abuse and having not spoken until the age of five. But for the grace of god, resilience and determination, she has risen above these obstacles to be successful. Munya is a strong advocate of personal responsibility and encourages people to make a real difference in their lives by creating lasting changes so they are healthy, whole and complete.

She envisions a kinder world where we treat ourselves and each other with dignity and respect. Her life purpose is to create better understanding and appreciation of Aboriginal people and to leave behind a legacy of Dreamtime wisdom for generations to come.

Stay connected

Sign up to our free Newsletter here at: https://www.evolves.com.au/ or download the following free articles

1. Talking Trees https://www.evolves.com.au/2018/11/28/talking-trees/
2. Who's Your Daddy? (Aboriginal Kinship) https://www.evolves.com.au/2018/07/27/whos-your-daddy/
3. The Dreaming of the Left-handed Kangaroo https://www.evolves.com.au/2018/11/28the-dreaming-of-the-left-%C2%ADhanded-kangaroo/

Personal Dreamtime Consultation

Would you like to find out more about Aboriginal Dreamtime? Perhaps you might like to discover your personal Dreaming or have it confirmed by Aunty Munya? Or, are you an alternative health practitioner wishing to learn more about bush medicine, healing practises and techniques?

You can have a personal Dreamtime conversation with Aunty Munya in person or by Skype. Book in for the special book price $699 (normally valued at $899).

To find out how, contact Evolve Communities at: https://www.evolves.com.au/ or email info@evolves.com.au

Aunty Munya as Speaker

Munya Andrews

Forwarded by Melbourne University as a 'leading Australian thinker', Munya Andrews is an accomplished Indigenous author and barrister with degrees in anthropology and law. Educated in Australia and the USA, Munya is fascinated by comparative religions, languages, mythology and science and intrigued by the way in which they interact and inform each other. Her book, *Journey into Dreamtime* is an easy guide to Aboriginal spirituality that explains Dreamtime concepts in a simple way.

Originally from the Kimberley region of Western Australia, she lives south of Sydney where she runs a business consultancy with co-director, Carla Rogers that specialises in Indigenous cultural awareness training. Over 7,000 people and 100 organisations have become more culturally aware with Evolve Communities. And that's just in the last two years!

Munya's life purpose is to create better understanding and appreciation of Aboriginal people and to leave behind a legacy of Dreamtime wisdom for generations to come. She is a highly sought after professional speaker that entertains, enthrals and captivates her audiences. She is one not to be missed.

You can have Aunty Munya speak to your organisation as a keynote speaker in a 60-90-minute presentation on one of the following topics:

1. Aboriginal Dreamtime
2. Traditional Healing
3. Songlines and Sacred Sites

www.ingramcontent.com/pod-product-compliance
Lightning Source LLC
Chambersburg PA
CBHW031129020426
42333CB00012B/303